CW01017634

THE
BRITISH
LIBRARY

a guide to its structure,
publications, collections and services

The British Library

a guide to its structure, publications, collections and services

Alan Day

Head of Department
Department of Library and Information Studies
Manchester Polytechnic

LA

THE LIBRARY ASSOCIATION

LONDON

Published by
Library Association Publishing Ltd
7 Ridgmount Street
London WC1E 7AE

First published 1988

British Library Cataloguing in Publication Data

Day, Alan Edwin
    The British Library : a guide to its structure,
    publications, collections and services.
    1. Great Britain. National libraries :
    British Library
    I. Title
    027.541

    ISBN 0-85365-628-2

Typeset in 10/12pt Palacio by Library Association Publishing Ltd.
Printed and made in Great Britain by Redwood Burn Ltd,
Trowbridge, Wiltshire.

'The British Library, in the quality and size of its collections and services offered or about to be offered to the public, has no parallel among other national libraries or among our own institutions.'

Viscount Eccles, Foreword to *The British Library Journal*, No.1

Contents

Preface

On a rough count some 550 titles are registered in *British Library Publications 1988 New Titles & Complete List*, ranging from catalogues of specialized collections to popular illustrated accounts of world famous heritage items. Many of these titles are indispensable to the effective operations of the library and information community and it has long been apparent that there was a distinct need for a descriptive conspectus. But it would be arid in the extreme to produce a disembodied review divorced from a coherent account of the British Library's origins, functions and activities. The Library occupies such a central position in the national library and information network that the whole institutional context needed to be presented. The sheer size of the British Library and its multifarious activities demanded no less.

And so the present work took shape. Fortunately that shape was conveniently close to hand, in that it made very good sense to adopt the British Library's own organizational structure as it emerged from its 1985 restructuring, and to describe the main functions and responsibilities of each division, so that existing and potential users might more easily understand how the different parts of the Library contribute to the national library service. There is a problem of nomenclature caused by the British Library's penchant for changing the names of its divisions and departments from time to time. Whilst every effort has been made to avoid anachronisms, sometimes this could only be achieved by descending into pedantry and, occasionally, common sense was allowed to prevail. Because of the strict limitations on space firmly imposed by the publisher, summary references are made to expert and authoritative sources of information. The alert reader will notice the significant debt also owed to the British Library's various newsletters and other ephemeral publications. Such readers will also note some apparent vagaries in citation and capitalization practice. The method of citing periodical articles is the one the author prefers, whilst capitalization simply follows what actually appears in the book or article referred to: in both instances the author is indebted to his editor for allowing him to stray from the normal house styles.

In compiling this book the author derived much comfort from the encouragement of Ian Haydon, Head of Press and Public Relations; Jane Carr, Head of Marketing and Publishing; and Peter Haigh, Head of Publications and Publicity Support Services at the Document Supply Centre. He is also indebted to Ann Norris, of the Publicity Office at Boston Spa, for tracking down archive copies of two illustrated brochures of the Urquhart Building. It hardly needs to be stressed that in no way can they be blamed for what follows.

Alan Day
Department of Library and Information Studies
Manchester Polytechnic
May 1988

Prologue
The birth of the British Library

That the British Library exists at all is remarkable: that this peculiar conglomerate of disparate institutions and enterprises has imprinted itself so indelibly on the national library scene in little more than a decade is really quite astounding. And, although the oldest of its separate components dates back to the eighteenth century, the British Library itself was brought into being with headlong speed once the impetus towards its formation gathered momentum during the 1960s.

It was the University Grants Committee's *Report of the Committee on Libraries* (HMSO 1967), the 'Parry Report', which initiated a thorough examination of the role of the British Museum Library and other national libraries. Elsewhere, the national library exercised many important functions affecting university library provision. Here, in the absence of a true national library system, these functions were shared by a number of libraries, including the British Museum Library (BML), inadequately resourced or equipped to undertake them. The *Report* urged that the BML should assume responsibility for the organization of interlibrary loans; the provision of foreign material, either alone or in cooperation with specialist and university libraries; and the immediate establishment of a national reference and bibliographical service. These new responsibilities could only be undertaken provided additional funding was forthcoming, and only when a new BML building was completed, and the library departments were reconstituted and housed as a unit.

The Committee's conclusions could not be shelved or ignored especially as the question of a new building for the BML was currently in the political arena. In December 1957 the Secretary of State for Education and Science appointed the National

Libraries Committee, under the chairmanship of Dr F. S. Dainton, 'to examine the functions and organization of the BML, the National Central Library (NCL), the National Lending Library for Science and Technology (NLLST), and the Science Museum Library in providing national library facilities; to consider whether in the interests of efficiency and economy such facilities should be brought into a unified framework; and to make recommendations'. Since the National Reference Library of Science and Invention (NRLSI), comprising the former Patent Office Library and the science collections of the BML, was administered as part of BML's Department of Printed Books, it too was encompassed in the Dainton Committee's terms of reference. The new committee immediately invited professional organizations and other interested bodies and individuals to submit written evidence; factual information concerning the adequacy and use of existing national library facilities was particularly required.

The *Report Of The National Libraries Committee*, Cmnd. 4028, presented to Parliament in June 1969, reviewed the background, functions, sources of finance, services, stock, staff, usage patterns and costs of the various libraries in the context of the United Kingdom's existing information network. The scene the Committee contemplated was not encouraging: 'Except in sharing a common aim to collect and make available information for which an existing or potential demand has been demonstrated, the many different library and information services do not at present form a well-ordered pattern of complementary and co-operating parts. Some units are large and have wide and deep coverage, but many more are very small, serving highly specialised needs.' Furthermore, 'even among the national institutions themselves, the variety of their administrative arrangements is not conducive to co-operation. Each institution enjoys either complete or a very considerable degree of independence from the others and from the other types of information service which it complements.'

The Committee's response was to recommend that a new statutory and independent public body, to be known as the National Libraries Authority, should be responsible for the administration of the BML, NCL, NLLST and the British National Bibliography (BNB). The BML should become the National Reference Library, and NRLSI should become the Central Science and Patents Collections, a separately administered unit within the

4

Authority. In detail, the National Reference Library 'should incorporate the library departments of the British Museum including the Department of Prints and Drawings, but excluding the NRLSI, and should be organized in the main as a closed access library' and 'continue to provide as complete coverage as possible in those subjects in the arts, humanities and social sciences where its present collections are uniquely good'. In the scientific area, the Central Science and Patents Collections, inheriting the NRLSI, 'should aim to provide a comprehensive collection of British and foreign patents, together with such technical literature as is needed to support the patent collection and to satisfy regional needs. This library should continue to provide for some time ahead direct access by its readers to a substantial proportion of its stocks.' Both collections should be located in Central London although not necessarily on the same site.

Recommendations concerning lending facilities were more complex: the loan stocks of NCL should be transferred to Boston Spa where a separate National Reports Centre should be established 'to collect, process and supply report literature in all subjects'. In special circumstances, lending from the National Reference Library, under carefully controlled conditions, was not ruled out, although this should not apply to material received by legal deposit or to items of high intrinsic value. To improve the effectiveness of interlibrary lending the highest priority should be given to bringing the union catalogues of the NCL up to date.

A new National Bibliographic Service should be established to combine, coordinate and develop the bibliographic activities of all the national institutions under examination. This service, whose main unit should remain in London, was also to assume responsibility for coordinating the total national bibliographic effort in science and technology including OSTI activities in this field.

Although the nomenclature employed by the Dainton Committee was not followed – no more was heard of the National Libraries Authority, the Central Science and Patents Collection, or of the National Reports Centre – the Government's decision to combine the BML, NCL, NLLST and BNB into a single organization, to be designated The British Library, fully accorded with the Dainton Committee's main recommendations. The creation of a unified national organization and the building of a new national library on the Bloomsbury site were announced in a White Paper, *The British Library*, Cmnd. 4572, January 1971. The objectives of the new library were defined as the preserving and making available for reference at least one copy of every book and periodical of domestic origin and of as many overseas publications as possible; providing an efficient central lending and photocopying service in support of other libraries and information systems; and providing central cataloguing and other bibliographic services. It would be necessary not only to build a new library in Bloomsbury but also to make further extensions at Boston Spa to house the NCL. An Organizing Committee would be appointed, legislation would be enacted, and the formal establishment of the British Library 'if Parliament approves', the White Paper concluded, would result in 'the creation of a national library system without rival. It will also provide in the centre of London the most significant complex of museums and library resources in Europe.' The British Library Organizing Committee held its first meeting in January 1971; the British Library Act, largely based on its deliberations became law in July 1972; and the British Library itself came into being on 1 April 1973.

The library was grouped in three Divisions: Reference (BML); Lending (NLLST and NCL); and Bibliographic Services (BNB and the Copyright Office). The Reference Division continued to comprise four well-established Departments: Printed Books (including the Map Library, the Music Library, the Newspaper Library at Colindale, and, from April 1974, the Library Association Library, as separate entities responsible for the collection of printed material in their own areas, the Official Publications Library reading room, and a Philatelic Collection); the Department of Manuscripts; the Department of Oriental Manuscripts and Printed Books; and the Science Reference Library (NRLSI). A Central Administrative Department provided the personnel, training, financial, administrative, staffing, accommodation and legal services necessary for such a large and complex organization. In 1974 the functions of the Office for Scientific and Technical Information (OSTI), previously located within the DES Scientific Branch, were incorporated into the Research and Development Department with responsibility for the promotion and sponsorship of library and information research in all subject fields. The India Office Library and Records were deposited on trust by the Secretary of State for Foreign and Commonwealth Affairs in 1982. Her Majesty's Stationery Office binderies at Colindale and Bloomsbury were integrated into the Library in the same year. In 1983 the British Institute of Recorded Sound was absorbed as the National Sound Archive and the Preservation Service was established as a separate department to be responsible for the overall direction and control of conservation and preservation processes for the Reference Division and for advice on the conservation problems of the Lending Division.

British Library's tenth anniversary in 1983 was rightly regarded as a suitable occasion to indulge in some modest celebration and to look back and take stock. Virtually admitting that a snag or two had been encountered in the early years – it could hardly have been otherwise considering the unlikely mix stirred together, venerable scholarship and automated document supply, the uprooting of one national library from the heart of academic London to some of Yorkshire's remotest broad acres – its evident pride and sense of achievement were nevertheless wholly appropriate.

'Ten years up', a special issue of *British Library News*, No. 87, July 1983, was given over to a record of the Library's major achievements: an automated information service, BLAISE, providing access to over 2¼ million bibliographic records; loans or photocopied articles in response to 25½ million requests; the establishment of a conservation branch which already had treated over 800,000 items; the promotion of research into the uses of new technology to aid the more efficient management of library services; and the acquisition of individual items of major importance to enhance its great reference collections. But the British Library has never been satisfied to rest on its laurels and far-reaching structural changes 'to allow the organization to provide services more efficiently to its many users' were effected in the Autumn of 1985 when 'it was thought timely to examine also the names of the Library's divisions and various units, and to change them to reflect this service commitment'. These changes were part and parcel of the Library's first Strategic Plan *Advancing with Knowledge*, published 21 October 1985, and are briefly sketched in 'Structure changes', *British Library News*, No. 111, September/October 1985:1 and 'Library announces name changes', *ibid.*, No. 112, November/December 1985:1–2.

Most significant was a reorganization of the Reference and

Lending Divisions into two Service Areas; Humanities and Social Sciences, and Science, Technology and Industry, which embraces the Document Supply Centre at Boston Spa (formerly BLLD) and Science Reference and Information Service (Science Reference Library). Bibliographic Services continues to be responsible for Record Creation and Automated Services whilst Research and Development's responsibilities remain largely unchanged. Four offices report directly to the Chief Executive: The Chief Executive's Office which provides corporate policy advice to the Chairman and Chief Executive; Corporate Finance, handling internal and external accounting policy and practice; Corporate Marketing, identifying opportunities for more services and coordinating sponsorship and consultancy activities; and Press and Public Relations whose tasks are to act as the focus for handling enquiries and to keep the publicity media informed of the Library's activities. A centralized Publications Sales Unit at Boston Spa fulfils orders for all the Library's publications except for printed publications issued by Bibliographic Services. The designations Division and Department were dropped as a matter of policy.

The purpose of this restructuring was to strengthen corporate cohesion in order to aid more effective resource management and service delivery, to exploit the Library's collections in the most effective way possible; and to focus services on the science, technology and business communities and on the humanities and social science community. To achieve this, working in cooperation with other libraries, and with the private sector, the functional objectives are enumerated:

1. to ensure the availability of a comprehensive and permanent repository of recorded British material in all fields, published or otherwise;
2. to ensure the availability of that foreign material which serves the needs at the national level for reference, study and information services;
3. to provide a centralized document supply service;
4. to provide the fullest possible range of information, bibliographic and other services to give effective access to the collections;
5. to create, distribute and provide access to bibliographic records giving a comprehensive and continuous account of

British and foreign publications;

6. to keep abreast of other library, archive and information resources both at home and abroad, and to establish such cooperative arrangements that will give users direct access or other appropriate reference to the widest possible range of material;

7. to identify priority needs for research and development in library, information and related activities, to provide support in these areas through funding research and demonstration projects; and to disseminate the results of the research;

8. to assist other libraries which are well placed to contribute significantly and at reasonable cost to the national collections as those envisaged in (1) and (2) above.

Since its formation the British Library has conscientiously issued at least seven A4 leaflets to illustrate its organization, each one more informative and comprehensive than its predecessor. The latest, *The British Library Structure and Functions*, a four-page brochure 'gives an overview of the organizational structure' and 'describes the main functions and responsibilities of each area to help existing and potential users understand how the different parts of the Library contribute to the provision of a national library service'. A front-cover chart provides an easy to understand at-a-glance outline of the new structure.

Part 1

British Museum Library
British Library Reference Division
Humanities and Social Sciences

History

The nucleus of the British Museum Library was the 50,000 volumes belonging to Sir Hans Sloane (1661–1753), physician, naturalist, antiquarian, traveller, President of the Royal Society, whose carefully drawn up will stipulated that his entire natural history collections; coins and medals; ancient, medieval and oriental antiquities; and library, should be offered in turn to the Crown, the Royal Society, Oxford University, and the Edinburgh College of Physicians, for the giveaway price of £20,000, one quarter of its estimated true value, to be paid to his two daughters. George II declined the offer on the grounds that the Treasury lacked the necessary funds whereupon the Trustees nominated by Sloane petitioned the House of Commons. After strong advocacy in favour of accepting the collections on the part of Mr Speaker Onslow, the Commons agreed to purchase the collections for the sum named and, with them, the Harleian Manuscripts, part of the great library formed in the first 40 years of the eighteenth century by Robert and Edward Harley, the first and second Earls of Oxford. To these two foundation collections was added a third: the Cottonian collection of manuscripts assembled by Sir Robert Cotton (1571–1631) which had already been acquired for the nation by the Cotton Library Act of 1700. It had been Cotton's life work to collect, to study and to provide access for other scholars to study the primary sources of English literature and history.

To meet the purchasing costs and to secure suitable accommodation, a lottery for £300,000 was authorized. An Act to incorporate the British Museum received the Royal Assent 7 June 1753. Headed by the Archbishop of Canterbury, the Lord Chancellor, and the Speaker of the House of Commons, 26 Trustees were appointed who then elected another 15 to their number. They were required to find a general repository within the cities of London or Westminster to receive the foundation collections. Free access to the collections was to be given to 'all studious and curious Persons'. Four years later George II presented the Museum with some 9000 books and 2000 manuscripts, collected by his predecessors from Edward IV onwards, and now known as the Old Royal Library. Along with this library came the privilege of legal deposit under the Licensing Act of 1662 and the Copyright Act of 1709 by which all British publications had to be registered at Stationers Hall in London. Nine libraries, including the Royal Library, were given the privilege of claiming copies of all books registered. The Trustees' finally decided on Montague House in Bloomsbury to house the Museum; it was acquired from the Earl of Halifax for £10,250; converted at a cost of a further £12,873; and opened to the public in January 1759.

It is not the intention here to follow in detail the 200 years' history of the British Museum Library until it merged into the British Library as the Reference Division in 1973. This is already well documented. Arundell Esdaile's *The British Museum Library a short history and survey* (George Allen & Unwin Ltd., 1946) covered its administrative history and includes details of the Library's more notable collections and their various catalogues. Edward Miller's *Prince of Librarians, The Life and Times of Antonio Panizzi of the British Museum* (Andre Deutsch, 1967) examines Panizzi's career in the Museum 1831–66 which witnessed the expansion of the book collections into a world-renowned research library. Panizzi's work at the Museum effectively touched all aspects of the Library's operations although his name is most often linked to the enforcing of the copyright laws (to the great benefit of the Library's collection development), and to the planning and building of the circular reading room and its surrounding iron bookstacks. J. Mordaunt Crook's *The British Museum a case-study in architectural politics* (Allen Lane The Penguin Press, 1972) is an authoritative account of the Museum's foundation and of its architectural and historical development. Graham Jones' 'The making of the British Library', *Library Review*, Vol 32, Spring 1983: 9–31 comments on the difficult times the Library experienced in the quarter of a century that elapsed between the end of the Second World War and the creation of the British Library when its influence and reputation within some sections of the library and information profession sunk to an unprecedented nadir. Peter Revell's 'Reference Division', *ibid.*, pp.35–44 is a thoughtful account of the Division's first ten years during which time an institution described as 'immensely inward-looking in the nature of the services it provided, which in general served the needs of its own immediate users' transformed itself into an energetic and dynamic library whose services to its readers have been extended and improved to a point where significant further advances are virtually impossible within its present accommodation. No longer is the Library 'a remote fastness' to which 'the average working librarian in a provincial university or one of the larger public reference collections. . . might refer an academic teacher who came to him with an insoluble bibliographical problem or an untraceable request' (p.36). BML's latter-day problems, management changes in Reference Division, and some informed crystal ball gazing, are all included in Alexander Wilson's 'The incorporation of the British Museum Library into the British Library' in *Studies in library management Vol 7* (Clive Bingley, 1982).

Reference Division's own perception of its functions was enumerated in British Library's *First Annual Report 1973–74*:

1. To collect, by purchase, gift and exchange, not only all British books and such British manuscripts and papers as are appropriate, but as much as possible of the world's important printed material in all subject fields, and manuscripts of foreign origin in certain specialist fields;
2. To make them available in the reading rooms to users who come to consult them;
3. To extend facilities to others by means of catalogues, photocopies, loans (to exhibitions), and information services;
4. To organize exhibitions exploiting the wealth of the collections for the benefit of both specialists and the general public.

To perform these functions the newly (1985) redesignated Humanities and Social Sciences now comprises five directorates. Collection Development exercises responsibility for the acquisition and record creation of material for the English Language, Western and Eastern European collections, Oriental collections, and the India Office Library and Records, whilst coordinating collection development throughout Humanities and Social Sciences. Public

15

Services provides reference and information services based on the collections and is specifically responsible for the General Reading Room, the North Library, and the Official Publications and Social Sciences Service, with a coordinating role for public services in the British Library Information Sciences Service and the Newspaper Library at Colindale. Special Collections supervises Western Manuscripts, Maps, Music and the Philatelic collections. National Sound Archive is the national centre for the study of recorded sound with listening and viewing facilities, and a reference library, whilst the Preservation Service is responsible for conservation and preservation operations.

Collection development

Department of Printed Books–The English Language, Western and Eastern European Collections

The translation of the Department of Printed Books, one of the British Museum's three original departments, into the English Language, Western and Eastern European collections may be a matter for regret, but nomenclature apart, its collections remain at the heart of the British Library. They include 200,000 volumes designated rare books which are kept under special security, and innumerable general and specialized collections acquired by gift, bequest or purchase since the Museum was established. A 28-page, paper-covered booklet, 145mm × 210mm, in the Reader Guide series, Alison Gould's *Named special collections in the Department of Printed Books* (1981) is a brief guide to these collections. Restricted to collections associated with a particular individual, in most cases the collector or a previous owner, which remain shelved together in the Library, the brief descriptive entries refer to any catalogues which may have been prepared or published and to other related printed material. A preliminary note covers the foundation collections.

Howard Nixon's 'Printed Books', chapter 12, *Treasures Of The British Museum* (Thames and Hudson, 1971) outlines the history of some of the more notable collections and illustrates some outstanding individual items. But Humanities and Social Sciences is not merely a book museum, it is the main beneficiary of the legal deposit regulations: with the exception of science and technology material which finds its way to Science Reference and Information Service, it receives a copy of every book and journal published in the United Kingdom. An annual grant for the purchase of printed material of research value in Western and

Slavonic languages, and English language material published overseas, upholds and vindicates the British Library's worldwide reputation for research and scholarship. Collection Development is too recent in origin for a corpus of literature on its functions and services to have emerged although R. J. Fulford's 'Department of Printed Books', pp.56–66, *British Librarianship Today* (L.A. Centenary Volume 1976) can still be read with profit. Janice Anderson's 'Department of Printed Books', pp.14–25, *The British Library, The Reference Division Collections* (BLRD, 1983) pays proper tribute to some of its more famous and illustrious items but does not fail to stress how modern technology is influencing its traditional services.

A BLRD Collection Development Group (CDG) was set up in 1983 to assist management to fix priorities in current and future acquisitions policy in a period of financial constraints. High on the Group's agenda was how BLRD's acquisitions could best be coordinated with other Divisions and how British Library's acquisition policy could take account of that of other large library systems. CDG was required to devise a set of collection development statements for BLRD's various Departments, all of which had their own well-established acquisition practices. This initiative may be regarded as one of the final moves to weld the British Library into a truly corporate entity ten years after its formation. The large-scale administrative reorganization the disparate units forming the British Library had experienced had not easily allowed for such fundamental reappraisal except on a Departmental basis. Not least among CDG's early tasks was to bring together whatever Departmental policy statements existed and to offer British Library users a better understanding of its overall acquisition policy and the contents of its multifarious collections.

A start had been made—many areas of the Library had issued guides, published catalogues were available, thousands of column inches in the professional press had been occupied by missionary descriptive articles—but it was sporadic and not subject to consistent or coordinated direction. To improve effective joint collection planning on a sound documentary basis CDG adopted the Conspectus system, recently developed by the Research Libraries Group of Stanford, California, which 'enables libraries to record and compare quantified data on the strength of their collections and collecting practices in particular subjects. It serves both as an information file and as a basis for collaborative collection development' (Stephen Hanger 'Collection development in the British Library: the role of the RLG Conspectus', *Journal of Librarianship*, **19**, (2), April 1987:89–107). Hanger reports that the British Library 'remains optimistic about the scheme as an aid to collection development. . . . Conspectus records now encompass the lending as well as the reference collections, thereby giving an overall picture of the level of resources and of their maintenance. For the first time, all collections and collecting policies are described and assessed in a single document'. The completion of the first phase of this exercise is marked by Brian Holt's and Stephen Hanger's *Conspectus In The British Library. A Summary Of Current Collecting Intensity Data Recorded On RLG Conspectus Worksheets With Completed Worksheets On Microfiche* (British Library, 1986).

Eighteenth Century Short-Title Catalogue
It was a Department of Printed Books initiative that transformed the concept of an eighteenth-century short title catalogue (ESTC), similar to A. W. Pollard and F. R. Redgrave's *A Short-Title Catalogue of Books printed in England, Scotland and Ireland. . . 1475–1640* (1926) and D. Wing's *Short-Title Catalogue of Books printed in England, Scotland, Ireland, Wales and British America. . . 1641–1700* (New York, 1945–51), into the realm of practicality. Long discussed in abstract (see R. J. Robert's 'Towards a Short-Title Catalogue of English Eighteenth Century Books', *Journal of Librarianship*, **2**, (4), October 1970:246–62) the project took a long step towards fruition at an Anglo-American conference, sponsored by the British Library and the National Endowment for the Humanities Washington, held at the British Library in June 1976, and attended by 40 librarians, bibliographers and computer experts, 'to explore ways and means of compiling a comprehenisve list of books and pamphlets printed in the English speaking world between 1701 and 1800' ('Start on cataloguing 18th century literature', *British Library News*, No. 7, July 1976:1).

General agreement was reached that ESTC should attempt to record as much material as possible within broad definitions, and that the record emerging should, as far as was practicable, conform to American patterns for large bibliographical databases. But the management of the project defied agreement. It was not until the Keeper of the Department of Printed Books announced that the British Library was prepared to sponsor a limited pilot project for six weeks that the necessary large institution support was forthcoming. The pilot project's terms of reference were 'to investigate the relative timings and efficiency of using the Reference Division's General Catalogue for a machine-readable base file for an S.T.C., in view of the unchallenged position of the Reference Division's collections as the largest single holding of English books. The project also had as its remit a study of the feasibility of using the same file as a base for retrospective conversion of the General Catalogue to machine-readable form.' The project's report laid down the ground rules which should be followed.

Much now depended on the extent to which the British Library could be persuaded to continue its involvement. Eventually the Director-General of the Reference Division confirmed the appointment of a consultant to undertake a second, more ambitious pilot project 'to develop further the necessary methodology; to establish routines for identifying the relevant works; and to draw up a practical set of cataloguing rules which could provide the library with records of its holdings compatible both with its existing printed catalogue and with computer catalogues of contemporary publications—the UK MARC files—held on the national database BLAISE'. To ensure that the bibliographical record would be as complete as was humanly possible all copies of an individual title were examined at the same time. Furthermore, to ascertain the full extent and range of uncatalogued items in the Library's collections, a six-week search was conducted of all volumes in the Department of Manuscripts thought likely to contain eighteenth-century printed material. Over 70,000 volumes and parcels were laboriously sifted through but the rewards were high: some 10,000 previously unrecorded items came to light. Three months work demonstrated the feasibility of a comprehensive recataloguing of the Library's eighteenth-century books, pamphlets and other material. The British Library Board agreed to fund a team of 15 cataloguers to complete this formidable task within an estimated three years and, in April 1977, what has been described as 'the largest single retrospective cataloguing operation ever undertaken' was successfully launched.

ESTC has progressed in two stages: cataloguing the British Library's eighteenth-century holdings and extending the database by incorporating records from other UK and overseas libraries. The first phase came to an end with the publication on microfiche of *The Eighteenth Century Short Title Catalogue. Catalogue Of the British Library Collections* in December 1983. An attractive illustrated 130mm × 240mm concertina prospectus heralded its arrival. Notes on its editorial processes, its scope and its three indexes (by date of publication; place of publication other than London; and by selected genres, advertisements, almanacs, songs, prospectuses, etc.) were all included. R. C. Alston's *The First Phase. An Introduction to the Catalogue of the British Library Collections for ESTC*, issued as a *Factotum* Occasional Paper, is a much fuller descriptive guide which reviews the project from start to finish. Alston's introduction provides a concise evaluation of the problems and issues, especially in relation to union catalogues, associated with the evolution of enumerative bibliography from traditional to computer application methods. An account of development overseas, the incorporation of the new records and locations discovered in a manual file at the British Library, and a synopsis of record structure and cataloguing practice, intended as a guide for general users, are also included. Work on the second phase—expected to last until the end of the 1980s—continues. *The Eighteenth Century Short Title Catalogue. The Cataloguing Rules*, last reprinted in a 1986 edition, is published to assist rare book librarians contemplating the automation of their catalogues. When completed, the ESTC will represent a resource of immense significance, and research into eighteenth-century political, social and printing history will be immeasurably advanced. As the file grows, records of material never before recorded, catalogued or located will become increasingly available. Alston's 'ESTC News. The Second Phase', *Factotum*, No. 18, March 1984:3–4 and No. 20, May 1985:3–4, report progress.

ESTC has always been well-documented. Nicolas Barker's 'An 18th-century STC', *TLS*, 3877, 2 July 1976:824, outlined the principal problems that confronted the Anglo-American Conference: the geographical distribution and nature of the materials to be included, the various methods to be adopted in compiling the catalogue, its dimensions and the project's staffing and finance. R. C. Alston and M. J. Janetta's early substantive work *Bibliography*

Machine Readable Cataloguing And The ESTC. A Summary History of the Eighteenth Century Short Title Catalogue. Working methods. Cataloguing rules (British Library, 1978) is described as a field report rather than a definitive history of the project although its account of its beginnings is detailed and authoritative. M. Crump and M. Harris' *Searching The Eighteenth Century. Papers presented at the Symposium on the Eighteenth Century Short Title catalogue in July 1982* (British Library in association with the Department of Extra-Mural Studies University of London, 1983) spotlights ESTC's research potential. Crump's introduction surveys the problems the project had to overcome and the methods developed to exploit records from contributing libraries.

R. C. Alston's 'ESTC six years on', *TLS,* 2 July 1982:726 stresses the British Library's contribution to the project: with ESTC on BLAISE-LINE researchers can now interrogate a file of some 140,000 bibliographical records in ways that no multitude of patiently compiled indexes could ever achieve. For the first time in the history of bibliography the truly curious have an opportunity to be gratified at what computers can and cannot do. '18th Century On-line', *British Library News,* No. 77, July/August 1982:1 estimates that 10 per cent of ESTC consists of items never before recorded. A parallel is drawn between interrogating ESTC and the central criminal index at Scotland Yard. The wonders of BLAISE's power to interpret intelligent searching are exemplified in Alston's 'ESTC Progress towards a bibliographical dream', *The American Trust for the British Library Newsletter,* No. 5, Spring 1982:2.

Factotum. Newsletter of the XVIIIth century STC, first issued in March 1978, was intended to appear quarterly although it has never consistently achieved this frequency. It was designed to give news of the activities and progress of the British Library team cataloguing the eighteenth-century books in the Library but since the end of phase one the emphasis has switched away from the British Library collections. An *Index to Factotum,* covering the first 20 issues, March 1978 to May 1985, compiled by Charles Wheelton Hind, has been issued. R. C. Alston's *Searching ESTC on BLAISE-Line* (1982), the first *Factotum* Occasional Paper, discusses the structure of an ESTC record, and attempts to guide the uninitiated researcher through technical complexities like search qualifiers and string searching. Alston's and J. C. Singleton's *Searching ESTC Online* (1982), Occasional Paper No. 2, demonstrates the sorts of questions that can profitably be asked of a machine-readable file. *The Eighteenth Century Short Title Catalogue*, a vivid red illustrated folded leaflet, 145mm × 210mm, introduces the project, indicates its coverage, enlarges upon its use to researchers, and signals the extent of its international cooperation.

Legal Deposit

Publishers' legal obligation to provide the British Library with a copy of all their publications distributed in the United Kingdom—books, periodicals, newspapers and magazines—derives from the Press Licensing Act 1662. Today legal deposit is embodied in section 15 of the Copyright Act 1911 as amended by the British Library Act 1972:

> The publisher of every book published in the United Kingdom shall, within one month after the publication, deliver, at his own expense, a copy of the book to the British Library Board who shall give a written receipt for it.
>
> The copy delivered to the British Library Board shall be a copy of the whole book with all maps and illustrations belonging thereto, finished and coloured in the same manner as the best copies of the book are published, and shall be bound, sewed, or stitched together, and on the best paper on which the book is printed.
>
> If a publisher fails to comply with this section, he shall be liable on summary conviction to a fine not exceeding five pounds and the value of the book, and the fine shall be paid to the British Library Board or authority to whom the book ought to have been delivered.
>
> For the purposes of this section, the expression 'book' includes every part or division of a book, pamphlet, sheet of letterpress, sheet of music, map, plan, chart or table separately published, but shall not include any second or subsequent edition of a book unless such edition contain additions or alterations either in the letterpress or in the maps, prints, or other engravings belonging thereto.

These regulations, with minor differences, also apply to the Bodleian Library, Oxford; Cambridge University Library; National Library of Scotland, Edinburgh; Trinity College, Dublin; and the National Library of Wales.

From time to time authors and publishers express a certain disenchantment that six copies of their books should be handed over *gratis* to these privileged libraries but, since 1950, their chagrin has been partially soothed in that each book received at the British Library's Copyright Receipt Office will be listed in *British National Bibliography*, widely used by librarians in book selection and book ordering procedures. Similarly, a record of music received finds its way into the *British Catalogue of Music*.

The principle of legal deposit depends on the distribution of each item to the public, not on its place of publication, or on the number of copies distributed. American academic publications, advertised and distributed in the United Kingdom, but not necessarily enjoying large sales, are a prominent case in point. Certain nondescript material – trade advertisements, passenger transport timetables, calendars, blank forms of accounts and receipts, and wall sheets for elementary instruction purposes – is exempt from the deposit regulations unless specifically requested.

A 95mm × 210mm folded leaflet, *Legal Deposit in the British Library*, explores the advantages of the deposit system, defines what constitutes a 'publication' under the Copyright Act, explains how the British Library is not concerned in any way with the ownership of copyright, and refers to three standard authorities for the interpretation of copyright law. Jean Mahy's 'The Copyright Receipt Office', *Bibliographic Services Division Newsletter*, No. 14, August 1979:3–4, is informative as is Richard Bell's 'Legal Deposit in Britain', *Law Librarian*, **8**, (1), April 1977:5–8 and **8**, (2), August 1977:22–6, which clarifies its effects on the British Library's collection building at different periods.

A legal deposit system for non-book materials is currently engaging discussion. Catherine F. Pinion's *Legal Deposit of Non-Book Materials*, a preparatory study carried out in response to a British Library request to examine the possibility of such a system, to indicate the problems involved and their implications for legislation, was published as a Library and Information Research Report in 1986. The main issues investigated were (1) what constitutes publication; (2) how adequate is current coverage in the United Kingdom; (3) the implications for producers and how many copies should be deposited; (4) the practicalities of legal deposit from collection and acquisition to accessibility; (5) what penalties should there be for non-compliance; (6) what the position was overseas and what problems had been encountered; (7) was the ideal solution regional deposit in a number of different organizations, if so what coordinating mechanisms would be required and under whose control; and (8) the role of the British Library.

Pinion's recommendations were that legislation should be extended to cover all forms of recorded knowledge couched in terms to ensure that all future information processes and methods of publication would be encompassed. The depository institutions should be permitted to transfer contents to other formats in order to preserve them and to guarantee access; deposit should be as comprehensive as possible with efforts to collect at regional level; the time limit for deposit should be the same as for printed material except for films where special arrangements would be required. Strong and effective penalties for non-cooperation would be required and publicity would be essential if a deposit system were to work effectively.

British Library's role was defined as providing a discussion forum, promoting the coordination of collecting non-book materials, urging the extension of the legal deposit system, and assisting in its enforcement. It should also encourage and facilitate the bibliographical control of non-book materials, encourage access to the collections, either by supporting the concept of regional depositories, or by the establishment of outstations to which material could be transmitted by land lines emanating from a central depository, and monitoring the effectiveness of the extended copyright legislation.

Department of Oriental Manuscripts – Department of Oriental Printed Books and Manuscripts – Department of Oriental Manuscripts and Printed Books – Oriental Manuscripts and Printed Books – Oriental Collections

Although the foundation collections of the British Museum contained oriental manuscripts and printed books the Department of Oriental Manuscripts was not formed until 1867 when there were great expectations, subsequently confirmed, that considerable additions would be acquired as British influence permeated throughout Central Asia. The new Department remained a sub-division of the Department of Manuscripts until it was enlarged to form an entirely separate Department of Oriental

Printed Books and Manuscripts in 1892. In 1983 the Director of the India Office Library was asked to undertake the direction of both Departments and its present title was assumed in April 1987. Oriental Collections (OC) hold the most comprehensive collection in the world of material in the languages and literature of Asia and those parts of North and North East Africa which use a non-Roman script, being particularly strong in the humanities and social and political sciences. Over 350 languages are represented in its holdings which are conveniently arranged in five geographical or cultural groups: Judaeo-Christian (Hebrew, Coptic, Syriac, Georgian, Armenian, Ethiopian); Islamic (Arabic, Persian, Turkish, Iranian and Turkic languages of Central Asia); South Asian (Sanskrit, Hindi, Urdu, Bengali, Tamil, Sinhalese, Tibetan); South-East Asian (Burmese, Thai, Vietnamese, Malay, Indonesian, Javanese); and Far Eastern (Chinese, Japanese, Korean, Mongol, Manchu). In the early years the acquisition and cataloguing of manuscripts predominated but with the supply slowly diminishing the importance of modern printed books in all the major Oriental languages is now reflected in the Department's acquisition policy. The greater part of its funds is now expended on current printed books although opportunities to acquire notable antiquarian items are by no means neglected.

Despite an inevitable emphasis on the wealth of its manuscript collections OC is not simply a haven for antiquarian scholars. In addition to the traditional areas of study, Islamic calligraphy and theology, Sanskrit literature, or Confucian philosophy, the collections are important for serious research in all fields of Asian or North African studies with the exception of modern science and technology material housed in the Science Reference and Information Service. The individual language collections require separate catalogues. After an initial general *Catalogus codicum manuscriptorum orientalium*, published in three parts, 1838–1847, all subsequent catalogues have been devoted to books in one language or group of related languages. These printed catalogues are accepted as authoritative works by scholars in the field. 'The Oriental Printed Books And Manuscripts', the last chapter of Esdaile's *The British Museum* (1946) describes the history, contents and provenance of the collections, and notes all existing catalogues. F. C. Francis' 'The Catalogues of the Oriental Printed Books and Manuscripts', *Journal of Documentation, 7*, (3), September

1951:170–83, lists those published to date in alphabetical order of languages.

The introduction to H. J. Goodacre and A. P. Pritchard's *Guide to The Department of Oriental Manuscripts and Printed Books* (British Museum Publications, 1977) places the collections in their historical context, emphasizes their artistic richness, looks at the Oriental Exchange Unit transferred to the Department to improve the acquisition of indigenous language publications, outlines reader and photographic services, takes notice of binding and conservation problems, and ends with a useful bibliography. The collections are described in alphabetical order of language arranged within four main geographical areas, Near and Middle East, South Asia, South East Asia, and Far East. Each entry gives the number of manuscripts and printed books included in a particular collection, their range and content, with details of published and unpublished catalogues. Some eye-catching illustrations and an index of languages complete a fully documented, scholarly but readable reference work. The scope of the collection is vividly imparted in K. B. Gardner, E. D. Grimstead and G. M. Meredith-Owens' 'The Department of Oriental Printed Books and Manuscripts of the British Museum', *Journal Of Asian Studies*, **XVIII**, (2), 1959:310–18.

More recently a number of A5 pamphlet guides for use in OC and the India Office Library have been published. Hugh Goodacre, Ursula Sims-Williams and Penelope Tusons' *Arabic language collections in the British Library*; Frances Wood's *Chinese language collections...*; Elizabeth McKillop's *Korean Language Collections...*; J. P. Losty and M. J. C. O'Keefe's *Sanskrit and Prakrit Collections...*; and Q. Mahmudal Haq and Salim Quraishi's *Urdu language collections...*, all follow a standard pattern: introductory sections to the history and nature of the collections of printed and manuscript material, with guides to specific collections, plus bibliographical references and notes on transliteration practice.

Albertine Gaur's 'Oriental Printed Books and Manuscripts', Chapter 9, *Treasures Of The British Museum* (Thames and Hudson, 1971) regards the collections not simply as a library but equally as 'a miniature museum of Oriental book art and Oriental ways of thought'. The same writer's 'Oriental Material In The Reference Division Of The British Library', *British Library Journal*, No. 2, 1976:120–32, is concerned to demonstrate that the British Library's material 'is much larger and more comprehensive than is generally realized'. In the wider view the Library's holdings can be divided into material written in Oriental languages and Oriental material written in Western languages. Gaur's expert eye passes over all categories of material associated with the Orient in the Departments of Manuscripts and Printed Books, in the Newspaper Library, in the Music Room, and in the Science Reference Library. Her *Writing Materials of the East* (1979), published in the British Library Booklets series, is an illustrated account of 'some of the items of great interest and beauty' in the Oriental Manuscripts and Printed Books collections.

G. E. Marrison's 'The Department of Oriental Manuscripts and Printed Books' in *British Librarianship Today* (LA, 1976) is a more prosaic account of the Department's collections, its public service, acquisitions, cataloguing and publication, conservation, and external relations. Janice Anderson includes a short but profusely illustrated outline of the collections in her *The British Library. The Reference Division Collections* (1983). A. R. Pritchard's 'An Index of Articles in The British Museum Quarterly On Material In The Department of Oriental Manuscripts and Printed Books', *British Library Journal*, No. 2, 1976:133–7, is arranged alphabetically according to language. A folded 89mm × 210mm illustrated introductory leaflet, *Department of Oriental Manuscripts and Printed Books* gives brief details of its history, collections and public relations. *Using The Oriental Reading Room*, an eight-page A5 pamphlet, is a practical guide to the collections, the catalogues, access to the collections and how to apply for material.

India Office Library and Records
The records of the Company of Merchants of London trading into the East Indies, more familiarly known as the East India Company, date back to before its incorporation at the end of the sixteenth century, and today number 175,000 volumes and files, comprising the archives of the East India Company (1600–1858), its Board of Control (1784–1858), the India Office (1858–1947), and the Burma Office (1937–1948), and constituting a unique and quite indispensable source of information on British trade in the whole South Asian area. Because these records are regarded as part of the Public Records of the United Kingdom they are made available to the public according to the provisions of the Public Records Acts.

In 1801 the Company founded a library as a public repository where its servants could deposit whatever books and manuscripts they had acquired overseas. These collections began to be regarded in the course of time as a reference library for Company officials and to acquire a wider reputation as a centre for oriental studies. Following the Indian Mutiny the British Government took over the administrative functions of the East India Company and established the India Office as a Department of State. The Company's Library became the India Office Library. In 1867 it gained the benefit of copyright legislation when the (Indian) *Press and Registration Act* required that a copy of every printed book issued in British India be sent to London. A selection process became necessary ten years later when the influx of material threatened to swamp the Library. 'As well as commercially-produced publications in English and in Indian languages, a vast amount of official material was received – reports on administrative, economic and political activity, encyclopaedic gazetteers and census publications, and the scholarly series of the linguistic, archaeological and other surveys' (Mary Lloyd, 'The India Office Library and its Collections', *State Librarian,* **25,** (3), November 1977:32–3).

When India and Pakistan won their independence in 1947 the receipt of books and official publications under the copyright legislation came to an end. The alarming effect this had on IOLR's collection building formed the basis of its memorandum submitted to the National Libraries Committee 20 years later. By this time the India Office Library, in common with the School of Oriental and African Studies, was unable to purchase more than a third of books published of significant research value. 'The provision which British libraries have been able to make in the South Asian field since 1947 contrasts strikingly with the provision made before 1947' by which date the India Office Library and Records had accumulated 'a virtually complete collection of official publications issued by the Central, Provincial, and State Governments of India'. The Committee was requested to designate the Library as the national library for South Asian materials and to recommend that its acquisitions of the current printed output of South Asia be restored to their pre-1947 levels.

Successive Government administrative changes saw the India Office Library come under the umbrella of the Commonwealth

Office, and subsequently the Foreign and Commonwealth Office, although it has always retained its former name. The posts of Librarian and Superintendent of the Records were joined in 1954 when the Librarian became Keeper of the Records, to be redesignated as Director of the Library and Records in 1971. After lengthy consultations between the Foreign and Commonwealth Office, the Treasury, the Civil Service Department, the Office of Arts and Libraries, and the appropriate trade unions, responsibility for the administration and management of the Library was transferred to the British Library with effect from 1 April 1982. 'A closer association of the Libraries should enable the British Library and the IOLR to combine resources to the best advantage of readers. Already it is agreed that IOLR will work with the other departments of the Reference Division' ('India Office Library and Records joins British Library', *British Library News*, No. 73, March 1982:1). That agreement was enshrined in a Policy Statement over the names of the Directors of the India Office Library and Records and of the Department of Oriental Manuscripts and Printed Books. 'There were obvious chances for rationalisation and co-operation which should be seized but both institutions were determined that whatever changes were to be made the services offered to readers should not deteriorate and, while resources might be redeployed, the range of acquisitions might actually be extended.'

Because the India Office Library was centred upon a specific locality which cut across the British Library's structure by function, language and form of publication, and because its collections overlapped with those of other departments, joint working parties were set up to decide policy in those areas where overlap or common interest existed. They were urged to keep constantly in mind the needs of readers and the prudent use of resources. The policy statement reported the working parties' decisions and recommendations. English language monographs 'was one of the difficult areas and there has been no proposal to alter the retrospective collections. . .although the IOLR will increasingly become the centre for purchase of antiquarian material dealing with the historical links between Britain and India. . . . The IOLR will not seek to fill expensive gaps which are already represented in the DPB's collections.' In respect to current acquisitions of English language material from India it became clear there was

30

scope for closer coordination: 'The actual mechanics of the complicated arrangements necessary are still being worked out in detail, but the range of publications available is more likely to be expanded than reduced, and duplication of little used books will be more effectively monitored and reduced.'

Overlap traditionally occurred in IOLR and OMPB with both departments holding substantial collections built up over a long period. The most intractable problem remained the major literary languages of the sub-continent, Bengali, Hindi, Sanskrit, Tamil and Urdu, where it was decided to monitor acquisitions to identify the amount of duplication. Responsibility for acquisitions in minor publishing languages was divided between the two departments. 'In the area of Islamic languages, IOLR will specialise in acquiring Arabic and Persian language material published in the sub-continent and will buy very selectively material concerning the sub-continent published in these languages elsewhere, leaving the major acquisitions effort in Iran and the Middle East to OMPB.' It was recommended that all periodical titles taken by IOLR should be reviewed to see if and where they were duplicated in other departments. 'In general it may be said that while economies will be made by the cancellation of some subscriptions, the overall position will not change significantly and coverage will not be reduced.' Newspapers did not present the same order of difficulty largely because neither the India Office nor the Newspaper Library collected vernacular newspapers to any large extent and so did not conflict with OMPB. No radical change was required in current policies and procedures for the acquisition of either Western or Oriental manuscripts although existing consultation between the India Office Library and the Map Library would be strengthened particularly in regard to antiquarian material. A simple line of demarcation was determined for official publications: IOLR would be the principal department for pre-1947 material with the Official Publications Library concentrating on material published subsequently. The working party on conservation effected a useful survey of personnel, equipment and resources of materials and recommended that consultation and advice be coordinated with the various workshops providing help and specific work in appropriate circumstances to other departments. Cataloguing practices posed some technical problems and it was decided 'that IOLR cataloguing data will be fed into the BLAISE/LOCAS system early in 1983...IOLR will need to adopt slightly different romanization practices in certain languages to conform to BL practice'. The policy statement is printed as 'Reports of the joint BL and IOLR working parties', *India Office Library and Records Newsletter*, No. 27, November 1982:1–3 and in *SALG Newsletter*, No. 21, January 1983:1–6.

IOLR's collection of printed books and serials in Western and Oriental languages totals nearly 4,000,000 volumes augmented continuously by an acquisitions policy aimed at obtaining all published works of serious research value in the languages of South Asia within its sphere of subject interest and of works in Western languages relating to the sub-continent and adjacent territories. Its newspaper and periodical collections, mostly in Western languages, include many unique titles of considerable historical interest not available elsewhere. Almost 30,000 Oriental manuscripts and 200,000 plus prints and drawings are also of immense research interest. Because of the wide range of unusual writing and other materials represented in its collections–palm leaf, birch bark, wood, copper, and precious metals, IOLR experiences daunting and intricate conservation problems as is evident in 'Conservation in the India Office Library & Records', *Library Conservation News*, No. 2, August 1983:1–3.

Essentially a research library IOLR is nevertheless open to the public although lending facilities are granted only to members recommended by employers, university teachers or other persons of recognized position who have known the applicant personally for at least two years. Members of the Diplomatic Services or foreign diplomats accredited in London are given readers passes on certified identification. Only printed books published within the last 25 years may be borrowed. Rare and valuable books, periodicals, bound volumes of pamphlets, and reference works on open access, are not available for loan. A 98mm × 210mm folded leaflet, *India Office Library and Records*, introduces its history, collections, publications and public services.

No doubt because of the wealth and diversity of its collections IOLR has been assiduous in printing catalogues and guides to assist readers. William Foster's *A Guide To The India Office Records 1600–1858* (Eyre and Spottiswoode for the India Office, 1919) opens with a scrutiny of the East India Company's administrative records and the reasons for their rapid growth. There follows a descriptive account of the records relating to the Home Administration, the administration in India and other countries, with sections on shipping and personal records. Joan C. Lancaster's *A Guide to Lists and Catalogues of the India Office Records* (Commonwealth Office, 1966), a 26-page booklet, is an overview of the many lists and catalogues to the various sections of the Records already printed and explains how these and other finding aids can best be exploited whilst her 'India Office Records', *Archives*, **IX**, (3), April 1970:130–41 lists and describes records accumulating in London, copies of Indian proceedings sent to London for information, records received at a later date through official channels, and other collections. S. C. Sutton's *A Guide to the India Office Library with a note on the India Office Records* (HMSO, 2e 1967) is an authoritative conspectus, of permanent reference value, of IOLR's European and Oriental books and manuscripts, drawings, prints, maps, photographs and other items. 'A Handlist of the Library's Principal Manuscript Collections; Publications of the Library; and Publications of the India Office Records' are included as appendices. The most detailed account, however, is Martin Moir's *A general guide to the India Office Records* (1988). Part 1 explicates the administrative background whilst part 2 is a descriptive inventory.

A set of free, brightly covered, A5-size printed pamphlet guides to various parts of the collections stand in a rack outside the Catalogue Hall of the Library. *The India Office Records* (20 pages) chronicles the historical background to the Company's archives, clarifies their geographical scope, and outlines the provision for their proper care and custody. An explanation of the general classification scheme in which 'all the principal archive groups or categories are distinguished by alphabetical references supplemented in some cases by numbers', precedes brief descriptions of the contents of each group which also serve 'to introduce the overall arrangement of the Records'. *Printed books in European languages* concentrates on the card and printed catalogues available and on the location of the various works of reference in the Catalogue Hall and in the Reading Room. *Official publications* reveals the type of document included in this category. *The map collections* surveys the origins and history of IOLR's collections and considers their scope, arrangement and finding aids. Related map collections in other institutions which supplement IOLR's holdings are listed. *Periodicals and newspapers* outlines the resources of the collections: 'Up to 1947 the subject coverage of serials in the Library and the Records included both the humanities and science, but since 1947 the Library has acquired selectively in the subject fields of the humanities, social sciences and economics, and has excluded law, science and technology. The Records have ceased to acquire serials, except to fill gaps in their holdings.' *Prints and Drawings* is a descriptive list of Western drawings, Company drawings made by Indian artists from c1787 onwards in a mixed Indo-British style, natural history drawings, Indian popular paintings, Indian miniatures, prints, photographs, oil paintings and sculptures.

The aim of Penelope Tuson's *Sources for Middle East Studies* is 'to bring together in a brief format all the information necessary for the new researcher who wishes to know the scope of the material...how it will be relevant to his or her studies, and how he or she can find a way into it'. Brief descriptions of quality, quantity and content of IOLR holdings are given with notes on the availability of indexes and other finding aids. *The European manuscripts* is a list of finding aids to the various collections divided into pre-1937 and post-1937 sections. Notes on the nature and scope of the collections, and the location of private papers elsewhere, are also included. *The Bengali collections*, *The Hindi collections* and *The Urdu collections* provide brief descriptions of their scope and give instructions on how to order material; lists of relevant reference works find a place. The same standard format is evident in earlier IOLR pamphlets, *Guide To The Sanskrit And Prakrit Collections*, *Guide To The Tamil Collections* and *Guide To The Tibetan Collection*.

The India Office Library and Records Newsletter commenced publication in January 1974: the first issue under the British Library logo, number 26, appeared in July 1982. Following the announcement that the IOLR and OMPB were to be jointly administered, it was decided to slightly enlarge the *Newsletter's* scope. *The India Office Library And Records Oriental Collections Newsletter* assumed its present unwieldy title with the September 1987 issue and is now normally distributed three times a year. News of current projects, notable acquisitions, reviews of new publications, details of research in progress, overseas visits by staff, colloquia and conferences, and longer articles based on items in the collections, are all regular features. A series of short articles on the work of IOLR's various sections began with 'European Printed Books section', No. 28, March 1983:1–2 and continued with 'The Map collection', No. 29, July 1983:1–2; 'Collections in the Prints and Drawings Section 1. Works by Indian Artists', No. 33, December 1984:3–6 and 2. 'Works by British artists', No. 35, June 1985:4–7. The activities of all sections of IOLR, readers services, conservation, photocopying services and staff publications, have been recorded in illustrated *Annual Reports* since 1983.

A. J. Arberry's *The India Office Library. A Historical Sketch*, first published by the India Office in 1939, and reprinted by the Commonwealth Office in 1967, tells the story of its beginnings and of the prominent personalities, not always at senior management level, who influenced its development and growth. An account is given of the provenance and history of some of the outstanding individual collections now in the Library. Rajeshwari Datta's 'The India Office Library. Its History, Resources, And Function', *Library Quarterly*, **36**, (2), April 1966:99–148, is an all-embracing survey of the Library before it entered the British Library; J. D. Pearson's 'The India Office Library', pp.176–8, *Oriental And African Bibliography. An Introduction* (Crosby Lockwood, 1966) is concise, factual and informative; B. C. Bloomfield's 'India Office Library And Records', *Herald of Library Science*, **22**, (1–2), January–April 1983:11–21 and *Pakistan Library Bulletin*, **XIV**, (1–2), March–June 1983:1–10, is an administrative history and an outline of its collections and public services. Janice Anderson's 'India Office Library And Records', pp.71–5, *The British Library. The Reference Division Collections* (BLRD, 1983) is an illustrated description of the Library's holdings.

Public services

General Reading Room

Famed for its circular design and 106 foot high dome, the present Reading Room, the seventh since the British Museum opened in 1759, was completed in 1857. Thirty thousand reference works are shelved on open access round the walls and on small bookcases at the inner ends of the rows of readers' seats radiating from the central enclosure behind two concentric circles of presses holding the main guardbook catalogue of the Humanities and Social Sciences collections and other large reference works and catalogues. Within each volume of the catalogue are two alphabetical sequences on each side of the open page with a third sequence on blue pages at the end of each volume accommodating entries for books received 1971–1975. The current catalogue containing entries for material received subsequently is on microfiche and may be consulted on readers placed to the left of a busy Enquiry Desk to the immediate right inside the main south entrance. Two special reading rooms are adjacent to the Reading Room: The North Library, a short corridor away, is reserved for the use of rare and valuable books; The North Library Gallery provides facilities for readers wishing to consult unbound periodical parts, microfilms or large-sized books. The Reading Room Annexe was opened in November 1987 to house national bibliographies and other substantial catalogues. 'Access is by the double doors on the East side of the Reading Room.' Information on admission procedures is printed in *Applying for a Reader's Pass*, a 98mm × 210mm folded leaflet. 'The British Library Reference Division is open to those who need to use material not readily available to them elsewhere, or who by virtue of their work or their research interests need regular or frequent access to the services of a research library.'

A series of Reader Guides and other informative leaflets and pamphlets are displayed in a rack near the entrance. *Notes for readers. A guide to the use of the Reading Room, the North Library, and North Library Gallery* (16 pages) advises on opening hours and regulations governing conduct in the reading rooms, how to find assistance in using them, how to obtain books and how to return them after use. An outline of the catalogues and indexes, notes on how to obtain periodicals, and advice on how to reserve books in advance come next before a list of other facilities, photographic and copying services, typing accommodation, sound proof cubicles, microfilm readers, and computerized information services. *The Reading Room*, a four-page leaflet, includes historical information, brief notes on readers' services, and various basic figures on the Reading Room's dimensions, stock and use.

The Reader Guides may be divided into two types: those relating to the efficient use of the catalogue, and those designated to assist readers in finding source material in specific areas of enquiry. *British and American authors* is a list with shelfmarks of bibliographies of English and American literature, guides to research, dissertations, biography, general indexes to periodical literature, and general bibliographies shelved in the Reading Room and the North Library Gallery. *Family and personal names. A brief guide to sources of information* is a similar list arranged under bibliographies, monographs–family names, monographs–personal names, and periodicals and series. Shelfmarks printed in italics indicate books on the open shelves. *British Family History. Printed Sources in the Department of Printed Books* includes information on the principal reference works, family histories, parish registers, biographical records, poll books and electoral registers, wills and guides. These are complemented by addresses of relevant libraries and record repositories and of societies concerned with heraldry and genealogy. *English Places. Sources of information* gives detailed notes on general works and bibliographies, the Victoria County History, directories, regional surveys, Domesday Book, buildings, place names, illustrations, and maps and atlases. Notes on newspapers and general periodicals, official publications, and calendars and registers of archives also find a place.

The Photographic Service undertakes to provide photographs,

photocopies, electrostatic prints and microfilms of books and manuscripts in the Library's collections subject only to the current copyright regulations and conservation inhibitions. *The Photographic Service at Bloomsbury* describes its facilities: what is available and how it may be ordered. To supplement traditional reference services a computer search service is offered by which a convenient print-out including an abstract or bibliographical references may be obtained. *Computer Search Service,* a foldover leaflet, explains how such a service works and describes the systems and databases available.

P. R. Harris' *The Reading Room,* published in the British Library Booklet series in 1979, is the most informative account of its history and present day functions. Generously illustrated, it discusses the British Museum's efforts to accommodate readers in its early reading rooms, enquires into the circumstances relating to the building of its present Reading Room, describes its construction and furnishing, sketches the personalities of some of the strong characters appointed as Superintendent, looks at the effect of the Second World War bomb damage, and rounds off the story with a step by step account of the procedures to obtain a reader's pass and a description of what the new reader can expect when he first enters the Reading Room itself. According to Byron Rogers' 'Writing Up The Reading Room', *Sunday Times Magazine,* 12 April 1987:56–7, 60, Mr Harris is currently engaged on a full-scale history of its traditions and folklore to mark its removal to the new British Library building on Euston Road. A less reverent glance at the Reading Room occurs in David Profumo's 'The cells of knowledge', *Literary Review,* No 69, March 1984:17–19.

General Catalogue of Printed Books
The General Catalogue of Printed Books is recognized as the nearest approximation to a universal bibliography there is of printed material in European languages. It forms 'a unique source for verifying citations, research and collection building of United Kingdom imprint material, rare and old books, pamphlets and papers'. The Reading Room working copy now fills over 2000 folio volumes incorporating all revisions and supplements until the British Library began to catalogue accessions in machine-readable form. The complexities of such a monumental catalogue are self-evident and are confirmed by the publication of R. S. Pine-

Coffin and R. A. Christopher's *How to use the catalogues*, a 24-page Reader Guide last revised in 1980. So daunting a document is this that the heretical thought crosses the mind that the untutored reader might well fare better by taking his chances and fearlessly approaching either the guardbook catalogue or the 362 volumes of the printed version in happy ignorance of the intricacies of such matters as entry point, choice and form of heading, corporate authors, and other arcane headings and sub-headings. No doubt researchers whose work frequently involves them in the unfathomed depths of anonymous books, for example, will be encouraged to learn

> One further complication occurs, particularly with older books. An anonymous reply to another work is entered under the heading appropriate to the original work, which may be anonymous. The entry for the second work will be found indented below the entry for the first. If there is an anonymous reply to an anonymous reply, it will be entered in the same place. NB. These rules have not been applied in the General Catalogue since 1972, when a somewhat modified AACR was introduced for books in this class.

Perhaps a trial and error approach is to be preferred. Other Readers Guides to assist the bemused reader are *Transliteration of Cyrillic* and *Special features of the alphabetical arrangement in Dutch books*.

In printed form the *General Catalogue* has experienced a chequered history. To confine the story to comparatively modern times:

> By 1920, the original catalogue and its supplement, having long been out of print, a new and revised edition was decided upon and was begun in 1931, in the hope that it would be complete in 12–15 years. By 1954, 23 years later, only 51 volumes of a projected 150 or 200 had appeared, and the rate of progress was such that an end could not be envisaged before many decades had passed.
>
> The Trustees of the British Museum therefore decided on a new method of production: to reproduce by photolithography the entries in the Museum's own working copy of the catalogue, thus eliminating all editorial work apart from the re-arrangement into one alphabetical sequence of individual entries.

Thus arose the edition of 1961–67 in 263 volumes. This edition has been out of print since soon after publication, and the new cumulated edition will avoid the need to consult (including supplements) several alphabetical sequences. ('General Catalogue of Printed Books', *British Library News*, No. 38, February 1979:1.)

A longer historical perspective may be found in A. H. Chaplin's 'The General Catalogue Of Printed Books, 1881–1981', *British Library Journal*, No. 7, 1981:109–19 and in his *GK 150 Years of the General Catalogue of Printed Books in the British Museum* (Scholar Press, 1987). 'The Author examines the peculiarity of the cataloguing system devised by Antonio Panizzi in the 1830s and gradually modified over 150 years, along with its relation to other cataloguing systems. He describes the production of three complete editions of the catalogue and two editions started but not completed and the controversies which surround them.'

The current catalogue, *British Library General Catalogue of Printed Books to 1975*, is published by K. G. Saur Ltd in 360 plus two unnumbered volumes. It consolidates into a single alphabetical sequence the *British Museum Catalogue of Printed Books* (263 volumes); *First Supplement 1956–1965* (50 vols); *Second Supplement 1966–1970* (26 vols); *Third Supplement 1971–1975* (13 vols); and 100,000 unpublished entries relating to material published before 1971 and acquired since 1975. 'The copy of filing and artwork is made up of reproductions of the 420,000 pages of the Red Books, which are the official work files of the British Library, containing pasted down sheets of the original main sequence of the British Museum catalogue and entries from the 1st and 2nd Supplements, together with bromides of the 3rd Supplement, and galley proofs of unpublished catalogue entries' (Introduction to Vol 1). The first six volumes appeared in the Autumn of 1979 and publication was expected to be completed by the end of 1984. In the event this forecast proved to be a trifle optimistic, the last volumes made their appearance in the early months of 1987. *British Library General Catalogue of Printed Books to 1975. Supplement*, to be published in six volumes 1987/1988, contains some 85,000 entries, relating either to titles published before 1971 but acquired and catalogued too late for inclusion in the main sequence, or reprints of entries now furnished with revised bibliographic detail.

40

Four volumes are devoted to *The Bible* in which entries have been arranged according to the languages of the original text. These four volumes *British Library Catalogue To 1975 Bible Sequence* are available separately as are two volumes of *British Library Catalogue to 1975 Liturgies Sequence* described as containing 'essential reference material for scholars who are concerned with the development of Christian liturgies both before and after the Reformation'. *British Library Catalogue To 1975 Russia Index*, volume 285 in the main catalogue, compiled with the help of the British Library's Slavonic and East European department, groups all Russian headings into the same volume and includes a specially prepared, entirely new and comprehensive index of sub-headings in the Cyrillic script, expeditiously guiding the user to the entry he is seeking despite the multiplicity of possible headings. This volume, too, is available separately. Regular users of the *Catalogue*, aware of the tortuous vagaries of the England headings, 'including every variety of publication imaginable, covering England, Wales, Scotland and, to a certain extent, Ireland and the Commonwealth', will appreciate the new BLC indexes to Titles and Subheadings, comprising two unnumbered volumes, which together form *BLC To 1975 England Sequence* in eight volumes.

It is inescapable that absolute currency can never be achieved in a catalogue of a continually augmented collection, and supplements become an unloved but inevitable necessity. *British Library General Catalogue of Printed Books 1976–1982* (50 vols) and *British Library General Catalogue of Printed Books 1982–1985* (26 vols) accommodate 1½ million entries and confine the gap in coverage within reasonable limits.

A long series of catalogues of incunabula, sixteenth- and seventeenth-century books in Western European languages, and of a number of special collections, all models of assiduous and detailed scholarship, has also been issued. They are listed and annotated in Arundell Esdaile's *The British Museum* (1946) and F. C. Francis' 'The catalogues Of the British Museum 1. Printed Books', *Journal of Documentation*, 4, (1), June 1948:14–40.

The *General Catalogue* is essentially an author catalogue; the first *Subject Index of the Modern Works added to the Library of the British Museum in the years 1880–1885* (1886) was followed by further volumes, usually published on a quinquennial basis although a single index was issued for 1961–1970. From time to time the possibility of larger cumulations, and even of retrospective volumes, was explored but the difficulties of such ventures were too great. A detailed bibliography of the Subject Index appears in the Preface to the *Subject Index of Modern Books 1971–1975* which concludes the series. F. J. Hill's 'Fortescue: The British Museum And British Library Subject Index', *British Library Journal*, **12**, (1), Spring 1986:58–63, looks at previous attempts to provide a classified subject catalogue and examines various methods of compiling a subject index. *The British Library General Subject Catalogue 1975–1985*, published by K. G. Saur in 75 volumes is the Subject Index's successor although in a different format and with a different approach. It represents titles acquired since 1975 in the former Department of Printed Books and some from the Science Reference and Information Service and Oriental Collections provided these have been recorded in the UKMARC database. Entries are arranged alphabetically based on subject headings assigned according to the principles of PRECIS (PREserved Context Index System).

Contracts were awarded in January 1987 to Saztec Europe Ltd, based in London and affiliated to a group of companies with long experience in catalogue conversion services to libraries in Australia and North America, for the conversion of the *General Catalogue* to machine-readable form, a project reported to be British Library's second most important objective ceding absolute priority only to its removal to the St Pancras building. The database will be keyboarded from the 360 volumes of the K. G. Saur printed edition and completion is scheduled to coincide with the first moves to the new building early in 1991. The converted catalogue will be directly accessed by users in the reading rooms and by remote users through BLAISE-LINE. It will also be made available on CD-ROM or other optical storage media. Not only will the *Catalogue* be one of the world's largest databases, links to an automated book ordering system will also give it a major role in the more efficient management of the St Pancras collections. 'British Library Catalogue conversion', *BS Newsletter*, No. 42, February 1987:1–2 outlines the project's dimensions whilst Pat Oddy's 'British Library Catalogue conversion', *ibid.*, No. 43, June 1987:4–6 sets the conversion into its historical context, examines the present Catalogue's form and structure, and discusses the processes involved in its conversion. D. W. G. Clements' 'Conversion of the

General Catalogue of Printed Books to machine-readable form', *Journal of Librarianship*, **15**, (3), July 1983:206–13 provides a more detailed account of the historical background, the imminent breakdown of the manual-based system of catalogue maintenance, the several aims of the conversion to machine-readable form, and of the problems to be overcome.

The State Paper Room – Official Publications Library – Official Publications And Social Sciences

From the mid-nineteenth century the British Museum Library has operated a policy of attempting to acquire a comprehensive collection of significant official publications of sovereign states and administrative territories. An extensive series of exchange arrangements was agreed with foreign governments and a wide range of official publications – books, documents and maps – was accumulated not only from the Dominions but also from the Colonies as a result of a Colonial Office instruction that the Library should be supplied with a copy of every Government document no matter how trivial. In 1931 the State Paper Room was created as a special division of the Department of Printed Books when official publications, previously scattered, were assembled together for specialist staff to exploit more effectively in a separate reading room. When the British Library was established the responsibilities of a renamed Official Publications Library were widened to encompass a reference service for the social sciences: sociology, health and welfare, education, public administration, politics and political history, modern history, economics, social anthropology and human geography.

A reference collection of some 2000 volumes, the principal parliamentary publications, and reference works on the official publications of other countries, has been on open access since 1974. Official publications still account for two-thirds of its use as is to be expected since Official Publications And Social Sciences (OP&SS) remains the only library which has consistently collected the entire printed output of the British Government, including ephemeral Departmental publications, not handled by HMSO, which often elude bibliographical control. Today's dual responsibility for official publications and the social sciences reflects the similarity of research demand: in both instances much of the documentation is not issued through normal book trade channels and bibliographical coverage is consequently exiguous. Fortunately OP&SS has been able to circumvent these inherent problems by virtue of its legal deposit privileges. Its collections are also enhanced by the deposit of archival material from government libraries whose prime function is to provide a current information service and which have little use for older and outdated documents. In addition OP&SS is a depository library for the United Nations and its agencies and also for the various European communities. Its growing importance in current information provision is confirmed by its computer search services and by its participation in the British Library's Business Information Service based at Science Reference And Information Service, for which it provides a back-up service for legal and statistical information.

A number of A5 pamphlets introduce OP&SS collections and services. *Using The Official Publications And Social Sciences Services Reading Room* is a brief guide to the collections and the procedures for ordering books. Information on the catalogues, the accessibility of the collections, and other services available, is included. *Parliamentary Papers. British Parliamentary Publications And Procedural Records Of Parliament in The Official Publications And Social Sciences Reading Room*, intended to help new readers to find specific publications, is useful in a wider context, identifying the entire range of this category of material, and remarking upon the various indexes and catalogues which act as entry guides. *Using Electoral Registers in The British Library* assists readers to refer to the electoral register collection, virtually complete since 1937. Historical complexities, caused by the shifting electoral boundaries, are clarified and the whereabouts of street indexes indicated.

A more substantial Reader's Guide, M. E. Goldrick's *Microfilm collections. Official Publications And The Social Sciences*, lists some of the Humanities And Social Sciences microform collections with notes on sets held by the Document Supply Centre at Boston Spa. Entries are arranged under broad area and country groups and the existence of a printed or filmed index to individual collections is noted. There is also a country (where appropriate) and a title index.

OP&SS compiles *Checklist of British Official Serial Publications* (12e, 1987) providing information about serials issued by UK central government departments, nationalized industries and public corporations. Entries show serial title, its issuing department, its frequency and how it is made available *i.e.* whether it has to be purchased or whether it is available *gratis* on request. An index of issuing departments and their publications is introduced in the latest edition. There are tentative plans for future editions to be issued at two-yearly intervals.

Stephen P. Green's 'The State Paper Room Of The British Museum', *Government Publications Review*, **1**, (1), Fall 1973:61–6 reviews its historical background and its operations, notably its acquisitions and records procedures, and describes in some detail its long established exchange network. Eve Johannson's 'The Official Publications Library of the British Library', *State Librarian*, **25**, (1), March 1977:6–7, 11 is more concerned with its 'new' functions and the ramifications of its enquiry services and the exploitation, actual and potential, of its collections. The fundamental difficulties under which it caters for a new user community are investigated and some searching questions are posed: 'What should be the relationship between the national library and other libraries? What should the national reference service be doing that it is not doing? What services are better provided elsewhere in the national library structure, and how far should the national library avoid duplicating these? What functions ought it to perform that some other libraries are at present performing?' 'Official Publications Library', *British Library News*, No. 67, August 1981:2 also spotlights its peculiar quandary: 'Special difficulties exist for the user and the librarian in retrieving material from the vast inadequately controlled field of official publications. The sheer number of documents issued means that potentially interested users can remain unaware of specific titles that are part of a large series as no library has the resources to catalogue analytically' and, further, 'The variety of government publications is not always generally appreciated. Typical searches might be not only for the familiar trade, social and political history, but for the social indicators for a future export market, innovations in public administration, or the background reasoning behind government decisions.' Janice Anderson's 'The Official Publications Library', pp.42–3, *The British Library. The Reference Division Collections* (BLRD, 1983) is a summary account of its resources and the importance of its collections.

Library Association Library – British Library Information Sciences Service

The British Library Library Association Library (LAL), at present located at Library Association headquarters, was formed in 1933 and was augmented by the Association of Assistant Librarians Students' Library of 1300 volumes in 1949. *The Library Association Catalogue of the Library* (1958) records library stock as on 1 March 1956. An account of the Library and its work shortly before the setting up of a Working Party on Association Services in 1971 can be found in L. J. Taylor's 'The Library Association Library', *Library Association Record*, **68**, (4), April 1966:123–9, 145. In its *Report* (1972) the Working Party noted that 25 per cent of the membership had used the Library within the previous two years but that its maintenance costs accounted for 28.7 per cent of the Association's subscription income. It was clear that the Library would increasingly devour resources the Association could ill afford. The remedy suggested was that other institutions should be invited to assume its costs on the grounds that the Library was of national significance. Following observations from 16 LA Branches and Groups, five of which recommended either merging the Library with another library or its transfer to some other institution, the Working Party discussed its future support with a number of outside organizations.

By far the most favourable response came from the British Library which stated its willingness 'to consider accepting the L.A. Library on deposit, to maintain and administer it as part of the British Library, and to guarantee to members of the Association the same services as they receive from the Library at present'. The Working Party regarded this as 'a particularly favourable offer and one which the Association would be unwise to reject'; the alternative was 'to allow the Library gradually to decline to a standard where it would no longer provide the services which the profession requires of it'. The British Library also guaranteed to maintain the Library in central London and, in the foreseeable future, in its existing accommodation. The Working Party recommended that the L.A. Council should approve the deposit of the L.A. Library with the British Library with effect from 1 April 1974 subject to the terms of a *Memorandum Of Undertaking Governing The Deposit Of The Library Association Library With The British Library* (Appendix 1, Working Party on Association Services: second report, *Library Association Record,* **75**, (12), December 1973:236–7). Accordingly the Library passed to the control of the British Library and was placed for administrative purposes under the Department of Printed Books. A brief survey of events and discussions leading to the transfer and its effects on the Library's services is included in L. J. Taylor's 'The Library Association Library and the British Library', *Library Association Record,* **76**, (7), July 1974:132–3. Advantages resulting from the transfer, how the Library contributes to the work of the various British Library divisions, and the possible effect on the Library's services once it moves to the British Library's new building, are briefly considered in the same writer's 'Central thoughts from librarians' central librarian', *Library Association Record,* **79**, (1), January 1977:23–5. The Library's continuing services to the library and information community are outlined in Sheila Corrall's 'Can I Help You?', *Assistant Librarian,* **74**, (10), October 1981:130–3, whilst her 'The L. A. Library's information plans', *Library Association Record,* **85**, (4), April 1983:145 examines various areas in which an urgent need for improvement in current information provision is perceived. Further details of this aspect of the Library's work are made clear in Roslyn Cotton's 'Information services in the L. A. Library', *Library Association Record,* **86**, (4), April 1984:174 and in her 'A Library for Librarians', *Assistant Librarian,* **77**, (7), July/August 1984:98–9.

A management review to quantify and cost the Library's services to the library and information services community in the areas of information, education and research was undertaken by Elizabeth Sparrow in 1985. She was also to identify overlapping resources within the British Library and to recommend how LAL could establish a resource allowing for a continuation of its basic services but also engendering fee income and sponsorship. Her report, *The Professionals' Library* (British Library, 1986) ends with a proposal that *The Memorandum of Understanding* should be renegotiated to take account of current service requirements and resources. A review of this report appeared in *Library Association Record,* **88**, (4), April 1986:184.

A measure of disenchantment on the part of the British Library, following the revelation that the cost of LAL's services was currently running at over £300,000 a year, was exacerbated early in 1987 when it became clear that it was facing a shortfall in grant-in-aid income as opposed to its total expenditure. Financial estimates prepared for 1987–8 pegged its allocation at £220,000. With forecasts for 1988–9 and beyond indicating further reductions British Library found it necessary to present the Library Association with alternative proposals to safeguard the Library's future:

1. To carry on with the present arrangements for the LA Library, but with a reduction in funding, including staff resources. Within this reduced funding the BL would practice economies by implementation of common stock policies and a major reduction in the acquisition of foreign language materials. The lending and consultation services would be maintained as far as possible (but the reduction in acquisition might drastically affect the usefulness of the Library); there would be little scope in the foreseeable future for the development of information services.

2. To subsume the LA Library collections within the broad collection development/public service area, to give up the separate reading room (or perhaps maintain a greatly reduced presence in Ridgmount Street), to follow BL common stock policies in general but with some duplication on demand and to operate a lending service to members from the Document Supply Centre at Boston Spa, while offering members full reading room access at Bloomsbury. At the same time as contractions or limitations were put in to effect the Library would begin to develop a special information service for the library profession, the book trade and other related groups. This would be based firmly in the services area, but would, with the opening of St Pancras, provide information services closely associated with the development of A Centre for the Book.

Either of these proposals, if accepted, would demand a radical revision of the *Memorandum*.

British Library favoured the second option: 'It offers rationalization of the conventional service with the positive promotion of information services' and 'gives the best chance of achieving flexibility, economy and efficiency' (K. L. Gibson, 'The professional's library: what's happening to it?' *Library Association Record*, **89**, (4), April 1987:164–5). In reply the Library Association took its stand on item 7 of the *Memorandum*: 'We pointed out firmly that the 1974 agreement provides for its amendment only by common consent' and, furthermore, 'there must be few parts of the British Library complex which were governed by such a legally binding agreement' ('Comment by the Chief Executive', *ibid.*, p.165). In this light, and in mind that the LA Library constitutes only a tiny proportion of the British Library's total expenditure, the Library Association requested the British Library Board to reconsider its position but agreed that it should draw up its own proposals for future funding. The Library Association's position was reiterated in 'Future of the L. A. Library', *Library Association Record*, **89**, (5), May 1987:219. Four main issues are identified in 'BL/LA Library: Working Group's proposals', *Library Association Record*, **89**, (9), September 1987:449–51. Agreement on the library's management and funding was signalled in 'Future of the BL/LA Library: draft agreement approved', *Library Association Record*, **90**, (1), January 1988:3. A renamed British Library Information Sciences Service will remain at Ridgmount Street pending its removal to the St Pancras building in 1993 and, in return for the Library Association reducing its rental and service charges (up to £35,000 per annum), British Library agreed to maintain the integrity of the existing collection and to keep it up to date within the framework of its current acquisition policies.

CABLIS (Current Awareness for British Library Staff), published monthly by the Library, first appeared in July 1975 after two trial issues had been circulated in September 1974 and June 1975. It was intended in the first instance, to encourage British Library staff to exploit the resources of the Library Association Library: 'We shall try to cater for the information scientist equally with the historical bibliographer.' Over the years the emphasis has changed—*CABLIS* must be one of the few acronyms to be given a new interpretation, since issue No. 49, May 1980, it has stood for *Current Awareness Bulletin For Librarians & Information Scientists*, in recognition that a far wider audience than British Library staff now receive it, but its arrangement and contents have remained essentially the same: a news section is followed by notes on new books, brief details of new periodical titles, selected journal contents lists, and selected abstracts from *Library and Information Science Abstracts*. Two indexes have been printed: *Index 1975–1980*, July 1975 to December 1980, compiled by postgraduate students at Liverpool Polytechnic, and *Index 1981–1982*, January 1981 to

December 1982, compiled by K. G. Bakewell.

Reading Lists, designed to provide a selection of references to the literature on topics of current professional interest, are available *gratis*. *AACR2* (1980) offers a selection of the more important contributions on AACR2 published in Britain, North America and Australia; a first supplementary list was issued in June 1981 and a second a year later. *Cataloguing in Publication* (1981) was compiled at the request of the Organizing Committee for the 1982 International Meeting on CIP and includes items which describe the development and operation of cataloguing in publication programmes and discusses the use by libraries of CIP data. *Charges for library services* (1980) is an updated version of an annotated bibliography originally prepared in 1979 for use by working parties of the Library Association and of the Library Advisory Council for England. *College Libraries* (1982) is an introductory list of references published in the United Kingdom since 1970. *Copyright* (1984) is a highly selective list, which reflects the enquiries received in the Library.

Data archives, machine readable data files and libraries (1980) looks especially at 'The Librarian's Role and Bibliographical Control of Data Files'. *Libraries and the new technology* (1980) should be used in conjunction with a First Supplementary List (1982). Both are divided into three sections: Library implications of New Technology; Studies of particular technologies; and Libraries in the future. *Microcomputers in libraries* (1983) is an abbreviated version of a bibliography compiled during a research project, *Microcomputer applications in academic libraries*, published as a Library and Information Research Report in 1983.

Reference services (1985), originally prepared for the British Library Research and Development Department, was made available because of the interest in a national electronic reference network. *School Libraries* (2e, 1984) is a select list on developments and current practice in the United Kingdom. It was first published in March 1982 with a supplement in February 1983. The 1984 edition includes material from both the earlier lists, with a substantial number of new references, in one sequence. *Government and Parliamentary Libraries in EEC Countries* (1980), a select list of books and articles, published from 1974 onwards, has been allowed to go out of print. Sparrow reported that many comments were forthcoming on these reading lists: although much appreciated they attracted criticism for being out-of-date and for not being sufficiently selective. She recommended that they 'should be expanded in a co-ordinated plan to cover all key issues of current interest. They should take the form of selective, annotated bibliographies and be sold.'

Notes for library users, *No. 1 Using The Library, No. 2 Photocopy service* and *No. 3 The Thesis collection*, assist first-time users to find their way round the Library's collections. Still in circulation is *Procedure for borrowing from the L. A. Library*, also numbered Notes for Library Users No. 1, which in fact contains much useful information on the Library's services and rules and regulations that has vanished from the later version. Details of the scope of the Library's collections, the types of materials held, its services and publications, a Library Directory, and a map of the Bloomsbury area, appear in a folded leaflet, *Library Association Library.* The Library has given notice that 'the search for the new name for the collection may mean that we allow certain publications about the use of the library to go out of print pending redesign and revision' (*CABLIS*, No. 120, May 1986).

Newspaper Library

Half a million volumes and 160,000 reels of microfilm of daily and weekly newspapers are housed in the Newspaper Library at Colindale, North London. The collections include English, Irish, Scottish and Welsh provincial newspapers from 1690; London dailies and weeklies from 1601; Commonwealth titles mostly acquired by copyright agreements with former colonial territories; 4000 volumes of nineteenth-century South Asian newspapers transferred from the India Office Library in 1986; and a representative collection from the rest of the world. *Newspapers in The British Library*, an illustrated 12-page, A5 pamphlet, introduces the collections at Colindale and the Burney Collection of London Newspapers 1603–1800, the Thomason Collection of Civil War newspapers, and the newspapers printed in Oriental scripts, all held at Bloomsbury. Finding directions and opening hours are also included.

As a self-contained unit with its own bindery and Reading Room the Newspaper Library opened 24 August 1932, replacing a repository which came into use in 1905. 'Colindale–50 Years On', *British Library News*, No. 78, September 1982:1; '1932–1982: 50

51

years service to readers and the public', *Newspaper Library Newsletter*, No. 5, Autumn 1982:1–4; and 'News from the British Library Newspapers–the Memory of the World. 50 Years at Colindale', *State Librarian*, **30**, (3), November 1982:36, look back and add detail. Gordon Cranfield's 'New Microfilm Reading Room at the British Library Newspaper Library', *British Library News*, No. 6, April 1986:2 features the opening of a sophisticated new microfilm reading room. Although additional premises were acquired close to the main site in June 1985 a storage problem persists, some newspapers are still housed in temporary sheds erected in 1940 after the original store was bombed.

'The objectives of the newspaper Library', *Newspaper Library Newsletter*, No. 8, June 1987:4 prints a four-point statement prepared to accompany its plan for the next ten years. In summary this reads: (1) To maintain the research collections of newspapers within the framework of the Library's collection development policy, including responsibility for the legal deposit of UK and Irish newspapers, selection of overseas newspapers, and microfilm purchasing to ensure the most effective use of preservation resources; (2) to provide the public services to exploit the collections and to act as a focus of expert knowledge of newspapers; (3) to ensure the preservation of the newspaper stock through planning the microfilming and binding programmes; and (4) to cooperate with other parts of the Division (i.e. H&SS) in assuring the most effective provision of services in the St Pancras building.

Following an internal report of the British Library Reference Division in 1976 a consultative paper, *The Newspaper Collections and the future*, invited comments from librarians, users and the newspaper industry on four crucial issues: the suitability of microform as a medium for the conservation of newspapers; the need to increase coverage of the principal British national newspapers and the desirability of retaining these newspapers in printed form for use by readers; the possibilities of improving microfilm equipment for library use and ways in which the Library could help; and the importance of retaining printed copies of the newspapers that have been microfilmed. As the British Library identified them the main options were to retain in remote storage all the pre-1950 foreign newspapers or to discard most of the post-1851 foreign newspapers except issues received via copyright agreements. After further internal discussions, and an analysis of the comments received, and subject always to the availability of the necessary funds, the British Library Board agreed that an enlarged programme of microfilming should be undertaken. Also, the Library would encourage the development of more suitable microfilm equipment, improve the facilities at Colindale, discard none of the printed newspapers after microfilming (a policy to be reviewed at intervals), purchase current foreign newspapers in microfilm wherever available and build an extension to the Library.

As part of the consultation process SCONUL (Standing Conference on National and University Libraries) recommended the establishment of a Working Party on Access to Newspapers 'to consider the most suitable arrangements for the coordination and the dissemination of information about the storage, microfilming and availability of newspapers and to make recommendations'. Its views on local archival responsibilities of libraries for the preservation and retention of British newspapers, a ten-point plan described as more of a code of desirable practice than as a rigid set of rules, along with a statement on British Library microfilming policy for newspapers, formulated in response to requests for financial support for local projects, were first presented in 'Two proposals for national cooperation', *Newspaper Library Newsletter*, No. 3, Autumn 1981:2–3. Subsequently the Reference Division funded a pilot study of the preservation needs of local newspapers, and how the British Library, in cooperation with local libraries, could support a comprehensive programme of microfilming or preservation. *NEWSPLAN: report of the pilot project in the South West* was published in 1986 as a Research and Development Department Library and Information Research Report.

In the following months NEWSPLAN assumed a more definite shape and its aims and objectives hardened as British Library, local libraries, newspapers and other institutions cooperated to identify needs and to agree on priorities. The programme now included

1. Research into existing preservation effort and the needs of libraries, museums and newspaper offices with the support of the British Library.
2. Sizing up the task of a preservation microfilming programme for newspapers UK-wide.

3. Establishing priorities, local libraries and the British Library Newspaper Library in cooperation.
4. Action to initiate microfilming programmes and to obtain resources for them.
5. Sharing experiences built up in the British Library on the management and technical aspects of large-scale microfilming.
6. Bibliography of British Newspapers assisted by the gathering of bibliographic and holdings information.

('Newsplan Update', *Newspaper Library Newsletter*, No. 7, April 1987:4–5.)

A world-wide review of the foreign collections, concentrating on current significant titles, has been initiated: Latin America, Australasia and Africa (French and English speaking) have come under special scrutiny. With the generous help of the American Trust for the British Library, extensive back runs of United States titles are being acquired to correct the deliberate decision taken by the British Museum in 1858 not to systematically collect American newspapers. At home the ambitious project of a national newspaper union catalogue, with the Library's records forming the base-file, is being seriously investigated. Following the donation of the *Daily Express* obituaries file, the Library is actively endeavouring to acquire similar collections: cuttings from the Royal Institute of International Affairs for the period 1940–1970 were accepted in 1984. Two series of information guides, provisionally titled 'Newsnotes' and 'Newsguides' are reported to be in the planning stage to provide readers with practical information so that the Library's services can be more effectively exploited.

The Bibliography of British Newspapers, originally a Library Association Reference, Special and Information Section project, will eventually cover all British newspapers in a series of historical county or counties volumes. The first to appear, *Wiltshire*, was published under RSIS auspices but subsequent volumes, *Kent*, *Durham and Northumberland*, *Derbyshire* and *Nottinghamshire* have been published by the Newspaper Library. Each newspaper is listed under current title if still published and unless specifically stated otherwise all entries represent weekly publications. Place of publication, publishers' name and address, details of complete files and their location in libraries, publishers' offices, record offices and museums, are recorded. Gaps in files are identified and microfilm holdings are also registered.

The Newspaper Library's working catalogue is kept in loose-leaf volumes and card indexes in the Bloomsbury and Colindale reading rooms. Dawn Olney's 'The Newspaper Library's Catalogue', *Newspaper Library Newsletter*, No. 7, April 1987:2 describes current cataloguing practices and procedures. A printed *Catalogue of the Newspaper Library Colindale. Vol 1. London; 2. England and Wales, Scotland, Ireland; 3–4. Overseas Countries; 5–8. Alphabetical by title* was published by British Museum Publications in 1975. 'The working catalogue of the Colindale collection, from which this version was produced was compiled for users of the library. Since readers usually require either a particular publication, of which they know the title, or the newspaper of a particular locality, it was designed to provide two sets of full entries, one arranged geographically and one alphabetically by titles' (P. E. Allen's 'Introductory Note', Vol 1).

Microfilms of Newspapers and Journals For Sale, an illustrated catalogue, is available *gratis. Newspaper Library Newsletter* whose purpose is 'to encourage an exchange of information about all aspects of newspaper collections' was first issued in August 1980. It was intended to be a twice-yearly publication but its appearance has been erratic.

'The Newspaper Library', pp.39–41, *the British Library, The Reference Division Collections* (1983) gives historical notes whilst John Westmancoat's *Newspapers* (British Library Reference Division, 1985) introduces British Library's comprehensive collections and indicates their value as primary source historical material. Alan Day's 'A Colindale Reverie', *New Library World*, **80**, (954), December 1979:238–40 is a highly subjective account of the Library's operations from the user's point of view. Its current problems and preoccupations, and its plans for the future, are outlined in Stephen Green's 'The British Library Newspaper Library In A New Era', *Journal of Newspaper and Periodical History*, **1**, (1), Winter 1984:4–11.

Special collections

The Department of Manuscripts—Western Manuscripts
Formed from the Cotton, Harley, Sloane and Old Royal Library collections the Department of Manuscripts was one of the original departments of the British Museum. Its collections now rank among the world's finest: religious and secular medieval manuscripts, Charters and Rolls, seals, Greek and Latin papyri, historical papers, literary manuscripts and autographs, immense holdings of music, maps and other topographical material, modern playscripts and photocopies deposited under the Export Licensing Regulations, are all encompassed. The Lord Chamberlain's Plays and Playscripts, an unbroken sequence of playscripts performed in Great Britain from 1824 to the present day, is a little known collection. Until 1968 plays had to be submitted to the Lord Chamberlain for licensing, but after the passing of the Theatres Act in that year, this requirement ended although a copy of every new play produced in Great Britain still has to be delivered to Western Manuscripts so that one copy at least is preserved. For all collections the aim has been to preserve and make available to researchers the written records of the world's intellectual and historical activities.

By their very nature manuscripts are necessarily and stringently restricted to readers undertaking research which cannot be carried out elsewhere and if they are to be exploited to their full extent they must be adequately recorded and documented. Writing in *British Librarianship Today* (LA, 1976) D. P. Waley remarked that the most difficult problems the Department faced centred round the compilation of printed catalogues. He was particularly concerned that the most recent *Catalogue of Additions to the Manuscripts* covered the years 1936–45 leaving a 30-year period of acquisitions recorded only in a 'Rough Register' issued by the List and Index Society, or in selective lists published by the Historical Manuscripts Commission. These problems were compounded by indecision as to whether the task of providing adequate catalogues for the earlier collections should be given priority over the cataloguing of current accessions. The dilemma is still unresolved: the most recent *Catalogue of Additions*, published in 1982, covers the period 1951–5.

In the absence of a complete catalogue of the Department's collections similar to the *General Catalogue of Printed Books* it is essential that printed guides be issued to the long series of *Catalogues of Additions* and to the catalogues of the named and special collections. T. C. Skeat's *The Catalogues Of The Manuscript Collections In The British Museum*, first printed in *Journal of Documentation*, 7, (1), March 1951:18–60, lists and annotates all catalogues in regular use, first indicating what types of material they cover. The most useful guide today is M. A. E. Nickson's *The British Library: Guide to the catalogues and indexes of the Department of Manuscripts* (BLRD, 2e, 1982), an A4, glossy semi-stiff cover, 24-page booklet listing both published and unpublished catalogues. The collections (and their catalogues) are arranged in order of acquisition except for live collections placed at the end. The contents of the printed *Catalogues of Additions*, i.e. all those acquired by gift, purchase or bequest since 1756, excluding those in the named collections, are displayed in tabular form. Catalogues of Charters and Rolls, Seals, Papyri and Ostraca, facsimiles and photocopies, and special interest catalogues, are also listed and annotated. An explication of the Amalgamated Index, a card index of names of persons and places, compiled from the indexes of the printed catalogues, situated in the corridor leading into the Students' Room, and a list of basic reference works shelved there, complete an admirably presented guide. Should your inclination be to add your own notes the wide inviting margins are irresistible.

A giant step forward came in 1984 when Chadwyck-Healey, after 20 years of close cooperation with the Department of Manuscripts, launched the *Index of Manuscripts In The British Library*. An index of persons and places containing over one million entries, published in ten royal quarto volumes, this is the first published listing in one alphabetical sequence of the Department's holdings. Search procedures for material accessioned up to 1950 are immeasurably improved, instead of 30+ indexes to consult there is now only one. The consolidated index includes all the indexes to the working catalogues although these sometimes lag far behind modern indexing practice. To ensure that the *Index* was finished within a reasonable time the accuracy and consistency of the entries was not checked although it was known that the older catalogues contained a number of errors. This fact is made clear in the introduction to the first volume although it finds no mention in the publisher's widely circulated brochure. Nevertheless the *Index* reveals the full richness and variety of the Department's collections and enables users to quickly identify individual items and the collections to which they belong.

Western Manuscripts is perhaps the least known of the British Library's public departments. The most comprehensive history and description of its collections, with brief references to whatever catalogues have been compiled, is Arundell Esdaile's *The British Museum Library* (Allen & Unwin, 1946) whose location on the Students' Room shelves is noted in Nickson's *Guide*. Both T. S. Pattie's 'Manuscripts', Chapter 6, *Treasures Of The British Museum* (Thames and Hudson, 1971) and Janice Anderson's 'Department of Manuscripts', pp.52–9, *The British Library. The Reference Division Collections* (BLRD, 1983) are beautifully illustrated accounts of some of the Department's most renowned items. *What to See: Manuscripts*, an A4 folded leaflet produced by the Exhibitions and Education Service in 1984, provides brief notes on 13 of these especially cherished pieces of history.

Department of Maps and Charts–The Map Room–The Map Library

The Trustees of the British Museum early recognized the need to provide appropriate facilities for readers wishing to consult maps. When the reading rooms were opened in 1759 a special table was appropriated for the large maps and surveys included in the Museum's foundation collections. Four years later there is mention of a Charts Room. The map collections were substantially augmented in 1828 when the library of George III, now known as the King's Library, was presented to the Museum. Some 50,000 atlases, maps, plans, charts and views from the King's Geographical and Topographical Collection were accessioned. From the mid-1830s, an active policy of collection building was embarked upon as the British Museum Library sought to acquire modern foreign maps by purchase and exchange. The collections were also enhanced by the acquisition of cartographical and topographical works relating to Canada, Australia and New Zealand through colonial copyright.

The growing importance of the map collections was signalled in 1844 when they were administered as a separate unit, from 1867 to 1880 as a Department of Maps and Charts, and as a sub-department 1880–92. Manuscript maps, except those in the Royal Topographical and Maritime collections, were then transferred to the Department of Manuscripts, and the Map Room was established as a division of the Department of Printed Books. By and large this structure still remains although the Map Library, renamed on the formation of the British Library, retains some manuscript maps acquired since 1892 judged to be of particular relevance to its collections.

The Map Library is the national repository for British map production, both past and present, and is the prime centre for cartographical studies. Most frequently consulted is the almost complete Ordnance Survey file including the surveyors' original manuscript drawings for the period 1793–1840, acquired in 1955. *The Original Manuscript Maps of the First Ordnance Survey of England and Wales, from the British Library Map Library* are available on microfilm from Harvester Press either as a complete set or in five regional subsets. The Library's information services include an open access reference library although its stock, some two million items–maps, charts, atlases, globes and aerial photographs–is on closed access. Well-established links with foreign survey departments and map producers ensure a steady influx of overseas material; more is received under exchange schemes. The Library's aims are to maintain world coverage on topographical scales appropriate to individual countries and regions and to collect all important general atlases and significant thematic or special purpose maps. Items of historic interest are acquired when opportunities arise. Outstanding acquisitions are noted, and often illustrated, in the British Library's *Annual Report*. A green and black foldover introductory leaflet, *Map Library*, contains notes on the collections, catalogues, services and admission regulations.

The *Catalogue of Printed Maps Charts and Plans. Photolithographic Edition to 1964* (10 vols, 1967) embodies the *Catalogue of the Printed*

Maps, Plans, and Charts in the British Museum (2 vols, 1885), and entries for accessions regularly printed for incorporation in the working copies of the *Catalogue* maintained in the reading rooms. The new edition was not a newly compiled work, nor was it uniform in the style and content of its entries: 'Since 1885, the methods employed in the descriptive cataloguing of maps have been progressively refined and elaborated, and cataloguing patterns of varying fullness and form may be seen side by side in the working copy. A thorough revision, however desirable, would involve years of delay, and would defeat the purpose of getting the *Catalogue* into print as quickly as possible.' Revision therefore took the form of modernizing and standardizing the form of geographical names used as headings. An Introduction provides notes on the *Catalogue's* scope and character; the selection and sequence of its headings and sub-headings; the order of entries; and on the descriptive nature of the entries. Maps and atlases, globes and related materials preserved in the Map Room and the more important cartographic items housed elsewhere in H&SS and in Oriental Collections are all included.

Corrections And Additions was published in 1968: six categories were identified, corrected entries, additions, deletions, corrected headings, locations of headings or sub-headings, and movement of entries. 'These Corrections and Additions are not claimed to be comprehensive. They are intended to remove certain internal anomalies which came to light at a stage in the process of reproduction too late for amendment to be made in print.' *The British Library Catalogue of Printed Maps Charts And Plans Ten Year Supplement 1965–1974*, (1978) is the first of a projected series of decennial supplements. 'Geographical headings have been revised where necessary in line with changes in the names of countries and other places made during the last ten years.' *The Catalogue of cartographic materials in the British Library: accessions from 1975*, available in the autumn of 1988 on 48× reduction microfiche, extends the bibliographic record.

Manuscript maps in Western Manuscript collections, and in the King's Topographical Collection, retained in the Map Library, are entered in the *Catalogue of Manuscripts Maps Charts And Plans And Of The Topographical Drawings in the British Museum*, (3 vols, 1844–61) reprinted in 1962. Although volume three was printed in 1861 it was never published having been destroyed by fire, so the reprint was made up from a surviving copy in sheet form. Manuscript maps accessioned later are entered in the appropriate *Catalogue of Additions to the Manuscripts* published since 1861.

A specially prepared British Library Map Collection offprint from *The Map Collector*, issue number 28, September 1984, in a semi-stiff pictorial cover, is described as 'a general introduction to the cartographic wealth of the British Library Reference Division'. Helen Wallis' 'A Banquet of Maps. An Account of the map collection of the British Library', begins the story in Tudor times, proceeds to the British Museum's foundation, brings the account up-to-date, and looks forward to the time when 'in due course all the departments now holding maps will probably be gathered together at St Pancras. . . . The future library may also hold such delights as the optical video disc on which, even at present, 56,000 graphic or map images may be stored and searched at will – the space-age equivalent of the seventeenth century atlas with its banquet of maps.'

Yolande Hodson's 'Maps of the Orient at the British Library' focusses on Chinese and Japanese topographical manuscripts. She reviews some of Oriental Collections' cartographical treasures, examines how they found their way to the West, and concludes 'the collections of the British Library are thus representative of the great diversity of Chinese and Japanese cartography up to the end of the nineteenth century'. Modern policies allow more systematic acquisition of material and today examples of topographical and thematic mapping of both countries are acquired when possible. Peter Barber's 'The Manuscript Legacy. Maps in the Department of Manuscripts' surveys a collection 'which stretches back to the dawn of Christian Europe, extends to the present, and is constantly being enriched with treasures for generations to come'. Andrew S. Cook's 'Maps from a Survey Archive: the India Office Collection' relates the history of the India Office Records from the foundation of the East India Company by royal charter in 1600, through its most flourishing period in the seventeenth and eighteenth centuries, the problems caused by a plethora of Indian surveys in the late nineteenth century, and to the dormant hiatus following the transfer of power to the new Dominions of India and Pakistan in 1947. The administrative history of the collections is also sketched. Sarah Tyacke's 'Useful Maps. Themes in European Geography' saunters through selected maps, placing them in their historical context.

Several other historical accounts of the Map Library's collections, detailing their scope and provenance, have been printed, notably R. A. Skelton's 'King George III's Maritime Collection', *British Museum Quarterly,* **XVIII**, (3), September 1953:63–4; 'The Royal Map Collections of England', *Imago Mundi,* 13, 1956:181–3; 'The Hydrographic Collections of the British Museum', *Journal of the Institute of Navigation,* **IX**, (3), 1956:323–34; and 'The Royal Map Collections', *British Museum Quarterly,* **XXVI**, (1–2), 1962:1–6. Helen Wallis' 'The Map Collections of the British Museum Library', the first chapter of *My Head Is A Map* (Francis Edwards and Carta Press, 1973), is a particularly well-documented study which surveys the development and progress of English cartography as a background to the Map Library's collections. Janice Anderson's 'The Map Library', pp.26–31, *The British Library. The Reference Division Collections* (British Library, 1983) is a short, illustrated survey of its services and collections. Skelton's 'The Map Room, British Museum', *Geographical Journal,* **CXXVI**, (3), September 1960:367–8 reports on its accommodation, staff, activities and acquisitions policy.

In accordance with the recommendations in the 1984 report of the House of Lords Select Committee on Science and Technology (Remote Sensing and Digital Mapping) the Map Library has assumed responsibility for making available on open access all forms of remote sensed imagery from aerial photography to multispectral data from satellite and airborne systems. Technical detail, and the archives available, are considered in R. P. McIntosh's 'Remote Sensing Resources at the British Library', *The Cartographic Journal,* **23**, (1), June 1986:68–9.

The Music Room–The Music Library–The Music Reading Area
Although printed music was included in the Old Royal Library presented by George II in 1757, it was not until the period 1838–56 that it became generally acknowledged that it required different treatment from books. Music literature was retained in the general collections but printed music was then assembled in a separate reading room. This arrangement continues to the present day: the Music Library collections are still mainly printed music although manuscript material is included in two important special collections that have been allowed to remain intact, the Royal

Music Library and the Hirsch Library. At the moment access to printed music and to music reference works is limited to the Music Reading Area in the Official Publications and Social Sciences Service reading room. Books and music periodicals may be requested in the main Reading Room in the usual way.

The collection of 1½ million items, covering the history of printed music from the early sixteenth century onwards, is incontestably the most comprehensive in the United Kingdom. Much has been acquired under copyright legislation although legal deposit has not proved so effective as with books and periodicals principally because of the absence of a music trade list which could be used to check the receipt of music in the Library. Filling the gaps in copyright material is regarded as essential if the Library is to achieve its ambition of holding as complete an archive as possible of music printed in the United Kingdom. But the Library does not restrict its acquisitions to copyright material, its purchases of new music published abroad are extensive and it can boast a wide selection of overseas contemporary music in addition to scholarly editions of older music.

In 1911 George V deposited the royal collection of music formed by George III and Queen Charlotte on permanent loan to the British Museum Library. Formerly known as the King's Music Library, and later as the Royal Music Library, it is noted for its autographed manuscripts, contemporary copies, and early printed editions of the works of Handel. A further 80 volumes of English church music, dating from the early eighteenth century, from the Chapter Royal St James, was added in 1926. To mark the bicentenary of the gift of the Old Royal Library Queen Elizabeth II presented the Royal Music Library outright to the British Museum in 1957. One of the conditions of deposit in 1911 was that a catalogue should be prepared and, after a long delay, caused by the First World War, the *British Museum Catalogue of the King's Music Library* was published in three volumes 1927–9. An historical account of the growth of the collection may be found in A. Hyatt King's 'The Royal Music Library And Its Collectors', Appendix A to his *Some British Collectors Of Music c1600–1960* (C.U.P., 1963). The same writer's 'English Royal Music-lovers and their Library', *Musical Times*, **XCIX**, (1384), June 1958:311–13 is equally informative.

With the help of a Treasury grant of £60,000, and a further

£50,000 from the Pilgrim Trust, the British Museum purchased the Hirsch Music Library for £120,000 in 1946. Assembled by Paul Hirsch, whose personal fortune derived from a family iron-foundry, the Library was removed to Cambridge University Library on long loan when Hirsch was forced to leave Germany in 1936. Strong in treatises and theoretical works published before 1800, full scores of operas, and early editions of the classics, the Hirsch Library was quickly re-established as an international centre for music studies. Its unusually complete collection of modern publications in sets replaced heavy losses from bomb damage during the war and it 'specialized in those very fields in which the Museum's collection of printed music happened to be weak' (A. Hyatt King, 'The Hirsch Music Library', *British Museum Quarterly*, XV, 1952:11–13). The full story of its acquisition and cataloguing is told in King's 'The Hirsch Music Library Retrospect and Conclusion', *Notes* (Music Library Association), **IX**, (1), June 1952:381–7. Hirsch himself published a *Katalog der Musikbibliothek Paul Hirsch Frankfurt am Main* (4 vols, 1928–47) but an extensive range of music literature had not been entered. This, along with musical works in volumes 2–4 of his *Katalog*, recatalogued according to British Museum Library practice, was included in a *Catalogue of Printed Music in the British Museum Accession Part 53. Music In The Hirsch Library* (1951).

K. G. Saur have completed publishing the *Catalogue of Printed Music in the British Library to 1980* in 62 volumes. 'For the first time a catalogue of a major music library of international standing is becoming available throughout the world to researchers, musicians, librarians and students' ('Music Catalogue launched', *British Library News*, No. 63, April 1981:1). This new catalogue unites in a single sequence the *Catalogue of Printed Music published between 1497 and 1800 now in the British Museum* (1912); Part III of the *British Museum Catalogue of the King's Music Library* (1929); 900,000 post-1800 entries mounted in the 'guard book' catalogues of the Reading Room; and the contents of numerous accession lists not incorporated in the main catalogues. But it is far from being simply a cumulation of earlier catalogues plus some additional entries: opportunity was taken by a joint editorial/Music Library team to correct some outstanding discrepancies in cataloguing practice. A 'Guide To The Arrangement Of Entries' is printed in the preliminary pages of every volume of the

Catalogue. O. W. Neighbour's 'Catalogue Of Printed Music In The British Library To 1980', *Brio,* **17**, (2), Autumn/Winter 1980:54–6 expands upon the difficulties of incorporating earlier catalogues and looks forward to the time when the *Catalogue* can be amalgamated with the *General Catalogue of Printed Books.* A. Hughes-Hughes' *Catalogue of Manuscript Music,* published in three volumes 1906–9 (*Vol.1. Sacred Vocal Music; Vol.2. Secular Vocal Music; Vol.3. Instrumental Music, Treatises etc*), covers all music manuscripts acquired up to the end of 1908. P. J. Willett's *Handlist of Music Manuscripts acquired 1908–67* contains brief descriptions of manuscripts held in Western Manuscripts and in the Music Library.

The British Catalogue of Music. A record of music and books about music published in Great Britain. . .based upon the material deposited at the Copyright Receipt Office of the British Museum, arranged according to a system of classification with an alphabetical index under composers, titles, arrangers, instruments etc. and a list of music publishers (BCM) was first published in 1957 by the Council Of the British National Bibliography Ltd in association with the Music Department of the British Museum, the United Kingdom Branch of the International Association of Music Libraries, the Music Publishers Association and the Central Music Library. Today the long sub-title has vanished, it is published unaided by Bibliographic Services, but it is still largely based on material deposited at the Copyright Receipt Office. Now, as then, music published abroad and made available through a sole agent, is also entered as are Music Library acquisitions bearing a post-1980 imprint. When first published the *BCM* excluded modern dance music and certain other types of popular music but from 1978 these categories have gained admission to enable it to become a complete record of music published in the United Kingdom.

Now compiled from computerized records, *BCM* appears three times a year, the third issue being an annual cumulation. Entries contain full bibliographical details and, from 1981, have been arranged according to the Proposed Revision of 780 Music based on the Dewey Decimal Classification *i.e.* by instrument or ensemble for which the work was written. Before that date the Coates musical classification was followed and, for the convenience of libraries who continue to classify their music collections according to Coates, the appropriate symbol is added to all entries. A composer and title index and, in the annual cumulation, a subject index, offer alternative approaches. A list of music publishers, formerly a regular feature, no longer appears. A cumulation, *British Catalogue of Music 1957–85* was published in 10 volumes K. G. Saur in 1987. Arranged in one updated continuous Coates classified sequence, 'this new publication will contain *c*60,000 entries and will include an index of composers, arrangers, editors, lyricists and titles, and a subject index in the form of an alphabetical guide to the classification scheme' (K. G. Saur publicity brochure).

Patrick Mills' 'The British Catalogue of Music: Inclusion Policy', *Fontes Artis Musicae*, **33**, (1), January–March 1986:28–9 contrasts the aim of a national music bibliography 'to represent the culture of the country concerned, in terms of scores composed, published (or available for hire in that country); settings of songs in the language of that country, and also music based on themes relating to that country', with the priorities of a bibliography based on the holdings of a copyright library *i.e.* 'to inform librarians what is available in a country, irrespective of its origins'. He concludes that *BCM* 'is not, and never has been, merely a catalogue of British music, but rather a music catalogue which happens to be British'. BLAISE-LINE introduced a new music database, an online version of both the *British Catalogue of Music*, and the catalogue of the British Library Music Library, in December 1987.

A 12-page A5 pamphlet, *Music in The British Library*, indicates the scope and breadth of the reference collections in manuscript and printed music, of the recordings at the National Sound Archive, and of the various printed catalogues. Information on lending services from the Document Supply Centre, and on research facilities, is also included. *Using the Music Reading Area*, an A5 eight-page guide, outlines the procedures for ordering books and music. In view of the present very cramped accommodation, sections on access to material and the printed catalogues, and a plan of the music reading area, are especially useful features. An A4 leaflet, *Music in The British Library Document Supply Centre*, calls attention to its 90,000 music scores, music periodicals, etc., and reminds users of how this important resource may be exploited. Hugh Cobbe's 'Music In The British Library', *Brio*, **23**, (2), Autumn/Winter 1986:59–64 is one of the first statements to emerge from any British Library section or division concerning the anticipated accommodation and pattern of public services once the St Pancras building becomes available. 'The realization of our goal of providing all our music services from one focal point, unencumbered by the burdens imposed by geography, supported by online catalogues and possibly by an automated book request system, should be achieved by 1994.'

Two well-documented works by Alec Hyatt King provide an authoritative history of the Music Library and a guide to its collections. *Printed Music In The British Museum, an Account Of The Collections, The Catalogues, And Their Formation Up To 1920* (Clive Bingley, 1979) examines the origin and growth of the collections, successive acquisition policies and the development of the published catalogues. *A Wealth Of Music in the collections of the British Library (Reference Division) and the British Museum* (Clive Bingley, 1983) is a selective guide intended as 'a work of ready reference, and a basis for further enquiry'. Information sources relating to the music collections in all BLRD departments are magisterially presented and documented. There are expert comments on the *Catalogue of Printed Music* and on the various catalogues subsumed within it. King's 'The Music Room Of The British Museum 1753–1953', *Proceedings of the Royal Musical Association*, 79th session, 1952–3:65–79 is a shorter but equally erudite survey of the collections. The administrative structure of the British Library's music collections is outlined in King's 'Music in the British Library', *Fontes Artis Musicae*, XXIII, 1976:101–2; O. W. Neighbour's 'National Collections', *ibid.*, XXV, 1978:205–6; and in 'The Music Library', *British Library News*, No. 84, April 1983:2. Janice Anderson's 'The Music Library', pp.32–7, *The British Library. The Reference Division Collections* (BLRD, 1983) and Arthur Searle's *Music Manuscripts* (British Library, 1987) are illustrated accounts for the general reader.

Philatelic Collections

Acquired entirely by gift and bequest, and by regular deposits from the Crown Agents and the Universal Postal Union; the Philatelic Collection is worldwide in coverage, and includes revenue material and fiscal stamps as well as postage stamps. Ephemera such as propaganda labels, new issue publicity hand-outs, exhibition vignettes, and a wide range of postal, telegraphic and customs stationery, enhance its value as a philatelic research centre. A massive Board of Inland Revenue Stamp Archive, deposited with the British Museum in 1966, extends back to 1710.

Bequeathed to the Museum in 1891, the Tapling Collection of some 50,000 stamps, including many rare and unique items, together with postcards, letter cards, stamped envelopes, registered mail and other items, may be regarded as the foundation collection. The main postage stamp reference collection, however, is the Universal Postal Union collection on permanent loan from the Post Office. Some 12,000 items are received annually from the UPU in Berne which distributes complete sets of all new postal issues from its member countries. Covering the period 1950 onwards is the Crown Agents collection, sets of stamps produced by the Crown Agents for their clients, enriched by artists' preliminary sketches, their final artwork, and stamp proofs. Other notable collections include three airmail collections, two collections of railway letter stamps, and the HMSO Collection of Excise Revenue material acquired on permanent loan in 1982. An illustrated concertina type leaflet, *Philatelic Collections* (1985) lists these and other collections, and also gives information on where and when items can be made available to students and research workers. Further historical notes can be found in 'The Philatelic Collection', pp.44–5, *The British Library. The Reference Division Collections* (1986).

R. F. Schooley-West, in charge of the Philatelic Collections, describes the different materials used, paper, ink and adhesives, and the difficulties the normal postal processes cause the conservator in his 'Philatelic Conservation Part 1–Historical Background and nature of the materials', *Library Conservation News*, No. 13, October 1986:4–5, 8. In Part 2 'Hazards to materials: prevention and cure', *ibid.*, No. 14, January 1986 (should read 1987):4–5, 8 he considers the physical, atmospheric, chemical and biological factors which threaten philatelic material of every sort.

'Major developments for Philatelic Collections', *British Library News*, No. 107, May 1985:2 made known an ambitious project to produce a complete inventory in the form of 33mm colour reversal film estimated to finally number 500,000 transparencies. Primarily this inventory will provide a reference point both for philatelic staff and for audit purposes and it will also be the starting point for the production of a manual catalogue. It is hoped that colour fiche of the Collections will be available for reference in the Reading

Room at Bloomsbury. The most informative overall view of the Philatelic Collections' activities is a 'Spotlight' feature printed in *Focus* (The British Library's Staff Newsletter), No. 15, January 1987:3−4 which deserves a wider circulation. Schooley-West's *Stamps* (British Library, 1987) is a lavishly illustrated introduction to the collections for the general reader.

National Sound Archive

British Institute of Recorded Sound

Frustrated by the absence of a national archive of phonographic recordings, Patrick Saul, founder and first Director of the British Institute of Recorded Sound, began to canvass support for such an institute during the Second World War. ASLIB was persuaded to call a public conference at Church House, Westminster, in 1947, which set up a Working Committee with Saul as Honorary Secretary. No money apart from a few hundred pounds from EMI and Decca was forthcoming but numerous meetings were held in the next few years at which a constitution was drafted and a policy initiated of seeking moral support from various educational and professional institutions by inviting them to nominate representatives to an embryonic governing body.

A financial breakthrough came when the Charles Henry Foyle Trust, a Birmingham-based Quaker organization, offered £2,000, the Arts Council granted £500 for three years, and the London County Council also promised support. A public appeal was launched for individuals to enrol as Friends of the Institute, to pay an annual subscription of £1 and to donate records. In 1953 audiences of several hundreds were attracted to a series of public lectures. Two years later the Institute moved into its first home, rented premises in Russell Square owned by the British Museum. By 1961 sufficient progress had been made to warrant an appeal to the Treasury which resulted in recognition grants of £10,000, £12,500 and £15,000 for the next three years. Since then grant-in-aid funding has continued. In 1966 the Institute moved to larger premises at 27 Exhibition Road, South Kensington.

The Institute was established to provide a comprehensive archive, international in scope, although predominantly British, of sound recordings of all kinds. Today the National Sound Archive (NSA) holds 750,000 discs, 45,000 hours of tape recordings, and a growing collection of specialist video materials. Although there is no legal deposit system for recorded sound media it receives copies of virtually every disc commercially available in the United Kingdom by virtue of the continuing goodwill of the British phonographic industry. As long ago as 1951 the Institute gave evidence in favour of compulsory deposit to a Departmental Committee of the Board of Trade then considering revision of the Copyright Act. When the Whitford Committee on copyright was formed in 1974 the Institute once more unsuccessfully argued that it should become 'a centre of deposit for two copies of all records manufactured for distribution in this country or imported for general distribution from abroad'. The Committee merely remarked in its 1977 *Report* that it was in favour of the establishment of national archives of films and published visual and sound recordings, but considered further investigation was required. In 1961 the BBC allowed the Institute to acquire recordings from its Transcription Service and to record broadcasts not otherwise made available.

Recorded Sound (1961–84) appeared as a quarterly until 1980 when it changed to twice-yearly publication. With a circulation of only 700 it was unable to survive but high quality articles on all aspects of the art and science of recorded sound, including Discographies of British Composers, subsequently published as offprints, found a place in its pages. General articles relating to the Institute included 'A Note on the Institute's new premises', No. 31, July 1968:308; Patrick Saul's 'A note on the Institute's prehistory', No. 52, October 1973:230–6; and Timothy Day's 'Sound Archives and the Development of the BIRS', No. 80, July 1982:119–27.

National Sound Archive

'British Institute of Recorded Sound joins Library as the National Sound Archive', *British Library News*, No. 84, April 1983:1 reported the latest stage in its history: 'It is hoped that the new arrangements will further interest in the work of the Archive whilst bringing it administrative benefits and the opportunity to share expertise on the preservation and care of archival material.' Clearly careful preservation of the Archive holdings must be accorded the highest priority. 'The main problems, most frequently encountered, are the intrinsic fragility of the carrier, the potential for chemical breakdown in the constituent materials, mechanical damage due to rough handling, inappropriate equipment or even from being played at all, and of course from adverse environmental conditions.' Fortunately, 'audio technology is such that it has for some time been far easier to produce a convincing authentic copy of an audio recording than it has, for example, of a medieval bible'. Fully aware of the delicate and unique nature of its collection, NSA has instituted 'a continuously researched long-term audio preservation programme', expertly expounded in Jeremy Silver's and Lloyd Stickells' 'Preserving Sound Recordings At The British Library National Sound Archive', *Library Conservation News*, No. 13, October 1986:1–3.

Together with the Mechanical Copyright Protection Society (MCPS), the British music industry's protector of copyright musical works on records, representing over 10,000 copyright holders in the UK and abroad, NSA is engaged on a centralized discography of all sound recordings. The National Discography is planned to be available online to subscribers by 1990 as a comprehensive computerized database of information on all commercially recorded material in the United Kingdom either currently available or deleted. 'The Archive plans to develop its services with the printed publication of the national discography, exploiting British Library's considerable experience in producing national catalogues of different forms of material. Work on the discography will also play an important part in plans to computerise the Archive's own catalogue of holdings' ('Work begins on national discography', *British Library News*, No. 14, February 1986:1). Malcolm J. Tibber's 'The National Discography Ltd', *Brio*, **23**, (1), Spring/Summer 1986:22–5 tells the story of its establishment from a different viewpoint, stressing MCPS's role as a single point of exchange for all recordings information but by no means overlooks the Archive's contribution to the joint venture: 'Many of the sound recordings required by the National Discography Ltd are already being kept at the NSA...much of this collection will be used in the compilation of the National Discography, which will, in turn, make it more readily accessible for public use.' NSA and MCPS are both featured in *National Discography. The Sound Recordings Bureau*, a glossy A5 pamphlet obtainable from National

Discography Ltd, Elgar House, 41 Streatham High Road, London SW16 1ER.

NSA's true position, somewhere between British Library and the BBC, is fully investigated in Christopher Roads' 'The National Sound Archive', International Association Of Sound Archives, UK Branch, *Newsletter*, 8, Spring 1984:13–16 where the whole field of non-music and non-human sound is explored, and the potential of sophisticated digital sound recorders and their processing is examined. NSA, in collaboration with Cambridge University's Engineering Department, and Cambridge Electronic Design Ltd, is developing what is described as 'a revolution in signal processing technology' *i.e.* Computer Enhanced Digital Audio Restoration (CEDAR) to eliminate disturbances inherited from master recordings, which have hitherto hindered the successful remastering of old recordings, by restoring disintegrating sound tracks and removing extraneous sounds. CEDAR is a low-cost digital signal processing software package which can unscramble the sounds of scratches and crackle caused by wear and tear. The electronic principles behind CEDAR, its range of applications, embracing every type of format and all kinds of audio signal, together with a diagram elaborating the various processes which make it work, are described in a pictorial A4 folded brochure *CEDAR Computer Enhanced Digital Audio Restoration*.

The British Library. The National Sound Archive, a four-page A4 pamphlet, outlines its collections, its listening and viewing services available by appointment, its comprehensive reference library, and its information service to help with preliminary research to locate particular recordings. Mick Brown's 'The sound collectors', *Sunday Times*, 29 December 1984 and Gillian Reynold's 'Lend them an ear', *Daily Telegraph*, 23 April 1988:xv add illuminating detail. A number of leaflets, all of which include a street map of the Kensington 'museum area', elaborate upon the specialized collections.

Western Art Music publicizes the Western concert tradition collection. 'New music from all parts of the world is particularly well represented. The most important source for recordings of new music is the BBC and the NSA provides the only public access to most of this material.' *Jazz and Popular Music*, constituting a significant proportion of NSA's holdings, includes 'a comprehensive range of commercially issued recordings in all styles from all periods; material in all formats, including wax cylinders, 78s, singles, LPs, tapes, cassettes, picture discs, flexi discs and compact discs'; and 'numerous BBC radio and television broadcasts by jazz and popular artists'. Interviews with musicians, writers and producers in the popular music business and record industry are also featured. *Traditional Music* mentions 'over 8000 LPs including complete sets of labels specialising in traditional music. . . rare and unusual LPs and cassettes of local manufacture purchased in the country of origin. . . a fast growing collection of unique unedited recordings from many different countries dating back from 1898 to the present. . . over 5000 discs from the early days of the record industry in different parts of the world. . .' and 'recordings of concert performances and workshops in the U.K. by visiting overseas musicians'. *Actuality & Documentary Recordings* indicates the type of material, and specific historical events available in the Listening Service whilst *Recorded Literature* highlights 20 years of live theatre performances, original poetry, prose and drama worldwide and BBC Sound Archive recordings. *Wildlife Sounds*, registers the importance of an old-established collection based on a great quantity of material bequeathed by Ludwig Koch, the German pioneer of wild bird sound recording. NSA's reference library which holds a wide range of catalogues and discographies, periodicals and monographs is an important documentary research source.

Two new reference works are planned for publication in 1988. *Directory of Recorded Sound Resources in the United Kingdom*, compiled by Lali Weerasinghe and Jeremy Silver, will contain over 400 entries relating to the holdings of libraries, museums, archives, county record offices, local radio stations, learned societies, sound recording groups and private individuals. *Popular Music Periodicals Index* (POMPI), to be published bi-annually, will be an easy reference guide to artists, groups and subjects from the major English language periodicals covering popular music.

NSA now offers a training programme: the principal course elements include establishing a sound archive; accommodation; selection and acquisition; copyright and public access; conservation and restoration; recording methodology (technical and procedures and practice); cataloguing sound archives; video recording; and public playback. Details may be found in a concertina type leaflet, *Training In Sound Archives*.

The Preservation Service

The British Library is confronting an appalling conservation problem, nowhere more visible than in Humanities and Social Sciences. 'Conservation of the Reference Division', *British Library News*, No. 19, July 1977:1–2 reported:

> The conservation of books and manuscripts in the British Library, always a necessary activity, has recently taken on a new urgency. The vastly increased usage of its materials in the last 15–20 years is perhaps the greatest single factor in the increased rate of deterioration. But there are other problems; the decay of bindings and paper due to coal smoke and gas lighting in the past and to modern industrial pollutants of all sorts, and the inadequacy of storage space and facilities in an overcrowded building are among the most serious.

A Preservation Service was created in 1983 when the HMSO binderies at Bloomsbury and Colindale were integrated into the Library. 'The decision was taken in principle to merge them with the conservation administration, the conservation workshops in the departments, and the photographic and reprographic facilities of the Reference Division to form a new Preservation Service, to be made the responsibility of an officer at Director level' ('Conservation and preservation', pp.13–16, *Tenth Annual Report 1982–83*). At the time it was the biggest organizational change in the Library since it was formed.

'Preservation–a new service', *British Library News*, No. 89, September 1983:1 starkly outlined the dimensions of the problem:

> From the unrivalled collection of 850,000 books published before the introduction of machine printing, perhaps 250,000 are in

need of conservation treatment which would take the in-house binderies 25–30 years to complete. In addition, hundreds of thousands of volumes of modern material have paper and bindings that are inherently unstable because of acid introduced at the manufacturing stage. The scale of the problem greatly exceeds any technical or financial resources that the Library possesses.

A glimpse of the work of the binderies prior to the formation of the Preservation Service is provided in Nicolas Barkers' 'Conservation in the British Library Reference Division', *State Librarian*, **25**, (1), March 1977:8–9. Today the Preservation Service is responsible for the control and supervision of the conservation and preservation requirements of the Humanities and Social Sciences collections, operating one of the world's largest conservation laboratories, and three studios, engaged with manuscripts and other special types of material, notably microfilming the brittle and yellowing newspapers at Colindale. 'Preservation Service marks first birthday with plea for more cash', *Library Association Record*, **86**, (8), August 1984:303 defines its attempts to contain the conservation problem.

F. W. Ratcliffe's '*Preservation policies and conservation in British Libraries: report of the Cambridge University Library conservation project*' (Library and Information Report 25, 1984) revealed an alarming lack of national coordination of preservation expertise, training facilities, funding and coordination of new preservation technologies. Cooperative action and a focal point for preservation activities in the form of a National Advisory and Research Centre, to be housed within the British Library, were recommended as the first steps towards an effective national preservation policy. An eight-page pamphlet, *Response of the British Library to Dr. Ratcliffe's Report*, followed and, shortly afterwards, the National Preservation Office (NPO) was established within the Preservation Service to promote the better conservation of library collections throughout the United Kingdom. It was announced that staff would 'visit libraries and preservation workshops, liaise with others concerned with preservation in archives, museums and educational institutions and establish an information database covering preservation practices and research' ('Library creates National Preservation Office', *British Library News*, No. 101, October

1984:1). An important part of the new service is the photography section whose day-to-day work, practices and procedures, and specialized work (ultraviolet and infrared photography, beta radiography etc.) are examined in David Jervis' and Graham Marsh's 'The British Library Reference Division Photography Service', *State Librarian*, **32**, (3), November 1984:33–7.

To mark the Library Association's annual conference in Harrogate, September 1986, whose theme was 'Preserving the Word', the Association and the NPO jointly issued *Preservation Guidelines*, a four-page, A4 leaflet giving practical information on the care of books and documents. Details on bookbinding and paper conservation courses, and a classified list of commercial suppliers of conservation materials emphasized its usefulness. Two subsequent leaflets consisting of short bibliographies of monographs, journal articles and other literature were issued with the intention that together they would form the basis for a general understanding of the implications of preservation for librarians. A revised version was issued by NPO a year later. *Permanent Paper*, an eight-page pamphlet published by the Library Association, NPO and The Publishers' Association, itself printed on long-life paper, is another basic document, giving answers to the questions 'What is permanent paper?' 'What is the problem?' 'What has happened in the United States?' and 'Is permanent paper available?' *Preserving The Word*, the conference proceedings, was published in November 1987.

Preservation: A Survival Kit, a set of ten coloured A4 size information papers of varying length, nestling in a laminated NPO wallet, was made available in the early summer of 1987. *Handling And Care, Cleaning And Repair, Storage And Display, Conservation Survey-Methodology, Disasters: A Survival Guide, Substitution Policy, Suppliers, Courses, Select Bibliography Of Printed And Audio-Visual Material* and *The Loan Of Archives And Library Materials To Exhibitions: Recommendations Of A Working Party* upheld the National Preservation Office's reputation for supplying basic and practical information. *Preserving The Past For The Future. The British Library's Commitment To Preservation*, a twice-folded A4 illustrated leaflet, 'describes some of the ways in which the British Library is not only combating the consequences of the deterioration of material but also trying to prevent such deterioration in the first place'. It also shows what help is available from the British Library for the preservation of other collections. Two A5 Preservation Guides, *It Just Came Apart In My Hands* and *See The Film And Save The Book* give cogent advice on how to handle books and details of the Preservation Services' conservation microfilming programme.

The NPO organizes annual seminars to focus on specific aspects of preservation. The papers of the first seminar, 'The Conservation Crisis–our Achilles heel', *i.e.* education both at library school and in libraries, have been published in book form as *Conservation Crisis. Proceedings of a seminar at Loughborough University of Technology, 16–17 July 1986.* A highly acclaimed video, *Keeping Your Words*, introduced by Magnus Magnusson and first shown on Channel 4 has been produced and can be purchased either in VHS (£7.50), U-Matic (£103.50), or 16mm (£632.50) format. Alternatively, it may be hired for £11.50 per week (all formats).

In an effort to attract additional funds the NPO has started the 'Adopt A Book Appeal', British Library's largest sponsorship scheme to date. *Adopt A Book And Save Our Literary Heritage*, a 95mm × 210mm folded leaflet, outlines the formidable costs of conservation, indicates what individual adoptions entail and suggests various schemes to raise money. Patricia Chapman's 'The Balloon Goes Up!', *Library Conservation News*, No. 16, July 1987:1–2 gives further details and reports on the April 1987 launch of the Appeal on the forecourt of the British Museum.

Library Conservation News, a quarterly newsletter, started life in April 1983 as a current awareness bulletin including news items, book reviews and article abstracts. A broadening of scope commenced with issue No. 8, July 1985, when articles taking a more reflective approach, and illustrated accounts of practical conservation, were introduced. Of particular interest are three reports: 'The British Library Overhead Photocopier' (No. 6, January 1985), 'Electroluminescent copying' (No. 8, July 1985) and 'Conservation copying: the Image Digitiser' (No. 10, January 1986) which describe new methods of conservation. A bibliographical curiosity is that issue No. 14 is wrongly dated January 1986. This should read January 1987. Patricia Chapman's 'The National Preservation Office', *Assistant Librarian*, **81**, (1), January 1988:6–8 relates the events leading up to its formation, its aims and concerns, its efforts to ram home its message at the local level, and its priorities in the immediate future.

Part 2

Bibliographic Services

British National Bibliography/Copyright Receipt Office–Bibliographic Services

Bibliographic Services Division (BSD) was formed in August 1974 when the functions of *British National Bibliography (BNB)* were united with a number of services and technical activities within the former British Museum Library, notably the Copyright Receipt Office (CRO). Its initial role was 'to process the acquisitions of the British Library for inclusion in its catalogues and other bibliographical services' (*The British Library First Annual Report 1973–4*, p.6). Six years later British Library's perspective of the Division's aims and objectives was considerably enlarged. Now its tasks were seen as threefold: 'To create bibliographic records and systems as a means of presenting a comprehensive and continuous account of the products of British publishers and of other publications, in forms that enable this account to be communicated effectively to the community of library users, and to assist librarians to provide effective resources and services in libraries; to provide services that enable bibliographic records to be effectively created, adapted and used within the British Library, and to be shared with other libraries; and to provide services that facilitate access by libraries and information agencies to records and data in information storage and retrieval systems' (*British Library Seventh Annual Report 1979–80*, p.43). In performing these tasks BSD has necessarily been in the forefront of automating and computerizing bibliographic records.

British National Bibliography had its origins in a 1947 Library Association committee which resolved that an organization should be set up to compile and publish a national bibliography and a centralized cataloguing service. The British Museum trustees agreed to allow books arriving at the CRO to be used for this purpose and to provide the necessary accommodation. After a prospectus had been circulated in 1948 to gauge potential subscriptions the Council of the British National Bibliography Ltd was registered under the Friendly Societies Acts in 1950 with a notional capital of 15 shillings (75p). Its early history is chronicled in 'British National Bibliography celebrates 21st anniversary', *The Bookseller*, 27 February 1971:1406–8, and A. J. Wells 'The British National Bibliography, 1950–1974', *Catalogue & Index*, No. 34, Summer/Autumn 1974:7–10.

The creation of BSD, its terms of reference, the services offered and its future plans are considered in Wells' 'New Patterns in Bibliographic Services: The Role of the Bibliographical Services Division of the British Library', pp.53–8, *Proceedings Of The Public Libraries Conference, Aberdeen* (Library Association, 1974). *BNB*'s role as a centralized cataloguing service is discussed in Andy Stephen's 'The British National Bibliography–aims and users', *The Bookseller*, 31 October 1986:1780–5. How *BNB* was transformed from a self-contained operation into a core element of a much wider system of bibliographic services is examined in A. H. Chaplin's *New Patterns Of National Published Bibliographies* commissioned and circulated to subscribers by BSD in 1977. BNB's Card Service is a diminishing part of its centralized cataloguing service. Information on availability, copyright, orders and prices is included in *BNB Card Service*, a leaflet issued by Bibliographic Services' Marketing and Support Group.

BSD's labours may be conveniently divided into three stages: the receipt of publications and the necessary cataloguing, indexing and classification to create the bibliographic record; publication of the records in printed or machine readable form; and the processing and supply of various related services. Its administrative structure is designed so that in creating bibliographical records of current English language material acquired by Humanities and Social Sciences, principally but by no means entirely by copyright deposit, a centralized cataloguing resource has been established which may be offered to other libraries, allowing them to dispense with costly routine cataloguing work and, at the same time, to keep up-to-date with the colossal number of books now being published.

Two major programmes, Legal Deposit and Cataloguing-in-Publication, ensure a steady flow of new and revised publications into British Library. The principle of legal deposit has been discussed in an earlier chapter; here it is important to note that new books and other printed material arrive at the CRO at a rate exceeding 300,000 items per annum. Newspapers are despatched to Colindale, serials for the most part go to Humanities and Social Sciences, and British imprint monographs, together with new and changed name serial titles, are initially sent to BSD. A sophisticated computer system, installed in October 1985, to enhance the efficiency of both the receipt of publications and the procedures for claiming material not deposited, is described in 'Automation in the Copyright Receipt Office', *BSD Newsletter*, No. 38, October 1985:5.

CRO's resources are also called upon by the United Kingdom National Serials Data Centre, established within BSD in 1974, whose prime function is to register serials on behalf of the International Serials Data System by assigning unique International Standard Serial Numbers (ISSNs) to currently published journals and forthcoming titles. By making use of legal deposit copies the Centre is able to assign ISSNs to newly published serials, including those which have changed their titles, before they are entered in *BNB*. Ross Bourne's 'The U.K. National Serials Data Centre', *State Librarian*, **25**, (1), March 1977:10–11 looks at its activities and background.

Cataloguing-In-Publication (CIP) is an advance information service about UK book and periodical titles for booksellers and librarians which came into full operation in 1977 after a pilot project had run in *BNB* throughout 1976. Its professionally catalogued and classified entries appear both in *BNB* and in the book itself. CIP is voluntary for publishers who are requested to provide advanced details of each new book: a copy of the title-page layout, a copy of the preface and/or introduction, whatever promotional material is available, an ISBN or ISSN, and a proposed publication date and price. The much vaunted advantages of CIP to librarians are the ability to place advance orders for new titles and also to process and circulate books quickly when they arrive using the limited CIP information for effective control until the full record becomes available. For publishers it offers a not to be missed opportunity to distribute records of new titles in printed form, microform, and through the electronic media in advance of publication. The whole operation is timed so that, ideally, printed CIP entries appear in *BNB* about two months in advance of proposed book publication date. Consumer resistance from libraries was evident at first: the view was expressed that a bibliography containing hard information about a book's publication was preferred to one offering no more than a vague promise about a title which might or might not actually be published. Nevertheless a project by the Centre for Catalogue Research, Bath University, over a six-month period 1981/2 reported that 90 per cent of British public and academic libraries made use of CIP records ('CIP widely used', *British Library News*, No. 76, June 1982:1).

A discussion paper, *Cataloguing-in-Publication: expanding the United Kingdom programme*, widely distributed to users of Bibliographic Services early in 1983, carried detailed proposals for improving the timeliness of UKMARC records. By and large these met with a positive welcome although specific queries included the adequacy of the incentives held out to publishers to gain their cooperation; current and potential backlogs; quality control; the inclusion of ISBNs; the lack of CIP information on price changes, the criteria and processes of revision of CIP entries; subject information; and the timing of the release data of CIP records (Michael Hamilton's 'Cataloguing in Publication – responses and comments', *BSD Newsletter*, No. 30, August 1983:1–2). Plans were put in hand 'to improve the timeliness of the UKMARC database, without loss of record authority and, second, to develop the UKMARC database, both as a valuable source of data for libraries, and as an effective aid for the marketing of British publishers' products in the library markets of the English-reading world' ('Cataloguing in Publication: the new programme set for take off', *BSD Newsletter*, No. 33, April 1984:1). The new style CIP records were introduced in January 1985.

Two promotional documents were circulated. *The Expansion of the UK Cataloguing-in-Publication Programme. Your Questions Answered*, a four-page, A4 brochure, to convince users on the benefits to be gained; saving time and money, reliability and an improved service to library users. *CIP. Cataloguing-In-Publication Handbook For Publishers* is a 16-page, A4 booklet, covering the scope of the CIP programme, the supply of CIP data, what the CIP Office requires from publishers, with brief notes on printing CIP data in books, data editing, changes to CIP data, legal deposit and guidelines for submitting titles to the Library of Congress CIP Program. Between them these two documents cover all aspects of CIP and set down clearly and concisely what exactly the current state of play is.

Introductory remarks in *The British National Bibliographic Service 1988*, an eight-page brochure, rightly claim that (1) it 'publishes an important range of bibliographies and bibliographic aids designed to serve many different user needs'; (2) 'The bibliographies offer the widest possible coverage of U.K. publishing output, and constitute a national bibliographic service of high quality records for selection, current awareness, reference and cataloguing'; and (3) 'The bibliographic aids include authorities and standards, and provide invaluable support to librarians concerned with both traditional and automated catalogue systems'.

British National Bibliography, is a weekly (i.e. 50 per annum) list of new books published in the United Kingdom and the Republic of Ireland, plus CIP entries for forthcoming books, arranged according to the 19th edition of the Dewey Decimal Classification, and catalogued according to the second edition of the Anglo-American Cataloguing Rules (AACR2). Some material is deliberately excluded: periodicals, except for the first issues of new or changed titles; printed music, recorded in *British Catalogue Of Music*; maps; and certain government publications issued by HMSO. Each issue contains an alphabetical index to the subject lists with entries under author, title and series. The last weekly index of each month includes two separate alphabetical author and subject indexes. January-April, May-August and annual cumulative volumes are published as are a series of quinquennial and triennial cumulated indexes and subject catalogues. Annual volumes from 1981 onwards are available in microfiche form. An *Author/Title Cumulation 1950–1984,* consisting of 500 fiche, presented in a compact case designed for permanent storage, was published after a sufficient number of advance orders were received before the end of April 1986. The *1981–1985 Full Cumulation,* offering subject, author and title access on 180 fiche, appeared in June 1987.

Radical changes are announced for *Serials in the British Library (SBL).* It is now a list of all serial titles acquired by purchase, gift or exchange, on a worldwide basis, in the British Library's two London-based reference collections, Humanities and Social Sciences and Science Reference and Information Service. In addition to author/title AACR2 catalogue entries *SBL* will now contain an alphabetical subject list derived from significant words in the serial title and will be published in three quarterly issues and a cumulative annual volume which previous to 1987 was only available on microfiche. From its first issue in June 1981 *SBL* also contained the locations and holdings of a number of other libraries, selected because of their geographical situation or of the significance of their collections, thereby converting it into a union list, although not on the same order of magnitude as its predecessor, *British Union Catalogue of Periodicals* but with diminishing resources this is no longer possible. 'New format for Serials in the British Library', *BSD Newsletter*, No. 41, October 1986:1–2 elaborates on all these revisions. *SBL*'s purpose of facilitating the use of serials within the library and information world, of satisfying bibliographic needs, and of meeting interlibrary lending requirements, remains essentially the same. Loans and photocopies from all titles listed in *SBL* may be obtained from the Document Supply Centre which will continue to list its own and some external library holdings in *Keyword Index to Serial Titles* and *Current Serials Received*. A cumulation of *SBL* on microfiche of all titles included since its first issue, in a single alphabetical sequence, also partly offsets the reduction in coverage. *Access to serials: Report of a working party by the British Library* (1978) and A. A. Mullis' 'Serials in the British Library', *BSD Newsletter*, No. 21, May 1981:1–2 provide details of *SBL*'s descent from *BUCOP* and of its scope, content and arrangement.

British Catalogue of Audiovisual Materials' 1979 experimental edition listed 5300 items: slides, filmstrips, spoken word sound recordings, tape slides and educational kits, based on ILEA's Central Library Resources Service. It is arranged in a Dewey classified sequence with an author/title and a subject index. A *Supplement* published in 1980 added over 2300 items whilst a further 1200 appeared in a *Second Supplement* (1983). *BCAVM* is also available for online searching as the AVMARC database through the BLAISE-LINE service.

The possibility of publishing major bibliographic cumulations in a medium other than conventional print, using micro-technology, was demonstrated when *Books in English (BIE)* was introduced in October 1970. Issued on microfiche at bimonthly intervals, cumulating progressively into an annual list, *BIE* is an author/title bibliography of English language books published worldwide compiled from the catalogue of the Library of Congress and *BNB*. A ten-year cumulation, *Books in English 1971–1980*, containing ten annual listings, together with the 1970 experimental records, in one alphabetical sequence, was published in 1984. Consisting of 600 fiche, listing 3 million entries, generated by 1.1 million English language titles, the cumulation is presented in a compact plastic case for permanent storage. The advantages in convenience of consultation of a complete decade's bibliographical records, dispensing with a number of cumbersome printed annual volumes, need no emphasis. A further cumulation, *Books in English 1981–1985*, was published in October 1987.

J. E. Linford's *Books in English*, a four-page A4 leaflet, offprinted from *NRCd bulletin*, August 1971, and his 'Books in English', *Library Association Record*, **74**, (1), January 1972:9 (different text) describe the original project in detail. *Books in English*, a BSD 205mm × 99mm fold-over leaflet, may still be available.

Also on microfiche, *The Bibliography of Biography* lists over 95,000 biographical works published worldwide 1970–84. Compiled from BSD's UKMARC file and the LCMARC file of monograph records, the *Bibliography* is arranged in two sequences: the main alphabetical name sequence and an author/title index. It is published in 40 fiche with a binder for permanent storage. Comments on its contents are included in 'Biographical revelations', *BSD Newsletter*, No. 36, June 1985:5.

Following *BNB*'s MARC Project in the late 1960s, when a small number of libraries tested the feasibility of producing a standardized machine-readable catalogue that could be manipulated and reformatted to service local practices and needs, *BNB* itself has been prepared from the MARC Service since 1971. Today, UKMARC, produced by Bibliographic Services, contains bibliographical records for all British books and first issues of serials published since 1950 and forms an online equivalent to *BNB* whilst AVMARC includes records for non-book materials issued since 1980 with special emphasis on audiovisual materials used in teaching. R. E. Coward's 'MARC Project', *Assistant Librarian*, **61**, (8), August 1968:174–5, his 'BNB and computers', *Library Association Record*, **70**, (8), August 1968:199–202, and 'Development of UK MARC services in the British Library', *R&D Newsletter*, No. 1, September 1974:1 narrate MARC's early history. Mindful of increasing confusion in MARC terminology–'it has come to be used variously to denote a method of processing bibliographic information, the format in which an automated bibliographic record is held, the structure by means of which bibliographic data are carried and transmitted for processing, the name of the bibliographic file or database in which bibliographic records are held, and the records themselves'–the British Library adopted revised definitions in respect of all the MARC-related services in the Autumn of 1987. An annotated glossary is included in 'MARC Nomenclature', *BS Newsletter*, No. 44, October 1987:3–4.

The *UK MARC Manual* (2e, 1980), a comprehensive guide to UK MARC format intended for all types of users–searchers wishing to know more about the MARC record, librarians and cataloguers interested in its bibliographic content or involved in record creation, and systems analysts exploiting the records in bibliographic or information systems, is published in a ring binder to permit page substitutions when required. Sections on magnetic exchange tape specification, exchange records, content designators and a cataloguer's manual of practice are included. A long series of Appendices deal with country of publication codes, language codes, geographical codes, physical descriptions, a key to AACR2 rules, changes to content designators from the previous edition and LC records reformatted to MARC. There is also a useful glossary.

A new phase in the British Library's exploitation of the MARC databases opened in January 1986. Instead of a close control policy based on the sale of records, rendered increasingly obsolescent by developments both in data storage and distribution technology, and in library automation generally, a more open policy has been adopted of persuading libraries to use to the full the immense central cataloguing resource represented by the combined British Library MARC files. By sweeping away outmoded restrictions on trading in MARC records and introducing an annual licensing system a total switch in emphasis has been accomplished: 'For libraries the main focus of our contractual relationships with the market for our cataloguing data moves from the wholesaler–in this case the bibliographic utility or database host–to the end user'; and 'the Licence fee is subscription-based rather than transaction-based. In effect this opens the door to new and more effective patterns of catalogue resource sharing and provides a framework for the exploitation of BL MARC records by new technologies' (Tony McSean, 'Licensing The Use Of British Library Bibliographic Records', *Vine*, No. 60, October 1985:15–21).

Three types of licence are now offered. The User Licence for libraries and other end-users of bibliographic records who require BL MARC records for permanent storage and in-house use. In essence any organization that holds a significant number of books needs a User Licence which enables the licensee to obtain BL MARC records from any licenced source and to redistribute them to any other licensees without restriction. By contrast the Library and Book Trade Utility Licences, both issued free, authorizes the licensee to distribute BL MARC records to any organization holding a User Licence and to operate an online database containing BL MARC records for purposes defined in the licence. The motive behind this change of policy is unashamedly commercial, in line with British Library's Strategic Plan which calls for a 25 per cent growth in earnings during the period 1985–90. At the same time there has been an easing of restrictions on the supply of bibliographic records to organizations within the EEC, entitling them to obtain BL MARC records from any organization within the network of Licence holders, using whichever supply system they prefer. Further background information may be found in 'Opening up record supply in the United Kingdom', *Library Association Record*, **87**, (11), November 1985:462–3 and 'Important News For Users Of BL Records', *BLAISE Services Newsletter*, No. 77, November/December 1985:1–2.

A warning note that Bibliographic Services' operations were fast overstretching its resources was clearly sounded in a major feature, 'The National Bibliographic Service and the UKMARC Resource', *BS Newsletter*, No. 42, February 1987:2–3 which set out significant factors in its strategic planning. British Library could no longer ensure it could cover its own catalogue and bibliographic control requirements, whilst simultaneously providing a national bibliographic service from the inadequate financial resources at its disposal. 'A significant reduction in the quantity and specificity of the descriptive and analytic content of the UKMARC record, though with no significant disturbance of the structural format' was predicted. What precisely was contemplated was clarified in a Consultative Paper, *Currency With Coverage. The Future Development Of The British National Bibliographic Service*, issued in July 1987. A 'Cataloguing Action Plan' with two aims was announced: 'to reduce current unit costs of cataloguing in the Library by 50% in order to handle current intake, to eliminate current backlogs and to anticipate the major increases in U.K. publisher output forecast for the 1990s', and 'to achieve compatibility of catalogue records created across the British Library, in order to aid the Library's own work and to widen the coverage of the British National Bibliographic Service'. To put this plan into effect a second or 'minimum level' of cataloguing treatment for modern English fiction, children's books, Science and Technology, items of 32 pages or less, and Religion will be employed. This 'minimum level' will be based on AACR2 first level of description supplemented with price and availability information. Further economies will be secured by discontinuing the application of Library of Congress subject data to *BNB* MARC records. Implementation of both measures is scheduled for 1988.

British Library's arguments failed to convince the Library Association which took its stand on 'the primary need to maintain the completeness of the bibliographic record in its present form'. Two crucial questions were asked: 'How does the British Library see the obligations of Bibliographic Services to the British Library itself as opposed to the profession at large?' and 'Is Bibliographic Services to be regarded as the cataloguing arm of the British Library rather than the successor to the former British National Bibliography Ltd?' ('LA response to the BL's proposal for the National Bibliographic Service', *Library Association Record*, **89**, (10), October 1987:539). Adding to the LA's 'extreme concern' were rumours circulating that British Library were contemplating giving up responsibility for *BNB* entirely. In correspondence at Chief Executive level British Library denied this, insisting that 'the sole object of the exercise...is to sustain the national bibliographic service at the best level of cost-effectiveness that we and the user community as a whole can achieve' ('Worse peril for *BNB*?', *ibid.*, p.495). The Library's proposals, modified as a result of representations received during the consultation period, were announced in 'Currency With Coverage', *BS Newsletter*, No. 44, October 1987:1–3. The responses received were described as having made 'an extremely valuable contribution to the planning of the future of the British National Bibliographic Service, which will lead to a vital and effective service for the 1990s'. 'Currency with Coverage Subject Indexing Proposals', *BS Newsletter*, No. 45,

February 1988:1–2 announces the implementation of the first phase of the Cataloguing Action Plan (*i.e.* that relating to the limitation of Bibliographic Services descriptive cataloguing) and outlines what it considers to be the basic features of the second, subject indexing phase to be undertaken 1988–1990 and planned in three stages: (1) the acceleration of PRECIS simplification; (2) the development of KWOC-type software for *BNB* and *British Catalogue of Music*; (3) the implementation of a new online interactive subject authority control system.

The British Library Automated Information Service (BLAISE) offered subscribers online access to a range of databases when it was introduced in April 1977. These comprised two distinct groups: the MEDLARS group, MEDLINE, SDILINE, TOXLINE, and several other biomedical and toxicological files of the United States National Library of Medicine, and the US National Cancer Institute; and the MARC group, UKMARC and LCMARC files, providing bibliographic records for monographs and first issues of periodicals published chiefly in the United Kingdom and United States. The two groups are now separately established as BLAISE-LINK and BLAISE-LINE, each operating independently. J. V. M. Bishop's 'Introducing BLAISE-Link and BLAISE-Line', *BSD Newsletter*, No. 25, May 1982:1–2 reports on the separation, outlines the databases available, and advises on access to the two services.

BLAISE-LINE continues to offer libraries, information units and the book trade, two major facilities: an online information retrieval service whereby users can interrogate its databases for specific titles to produce booklists, bibliographies or current awareness material, covering all subject areas; and the facility to identify and retrieval high quality bibliographic records. Besides BNBMARC and LCMARC (bibliographic records for all monographs acquired by the US Library of Congress since 1968), the database files available include British Library Catalogue (BLC); Document Supply Centre monographs in Western European languages published since 1980; BLC Humanities and Social Sciences acquisitions since 1976 together with those of Oriental Collections since 1980 and non-archival materials of the India Office Library from 1983; BLC Science Reference and Information Service acquisitions from 1974, including a complete listing of SRIS periodical holdings; and the University of London Catalogue. J. Whitaker & Sons' *British Books in Print* file, updated monthly, and containing brief records of British books and English-language titles published overseas but available in the United Kingdom through a sole stock-holding supplier, contributes up-to-the-minute information on price and availability that BNBMARC lacks. Conference Proceedings Index which covers the proceedings of conferences, symposia, seminars and workshops, principally from 1964 onwards, and SIGLE, are also available. So too are AVMARC and the Music Library Catalogue. For antiquarian material the Incunable Short Title Catalogue, a worldwide listing of bibliographic records for all types of material printed with moveable type before 1501, and the Eighteenth Century Short Title Catalogue, can be utilized..

BSD is currently looking further ahead with its BLAISE System 2 project whereby its existing software for BLAISE-LINE will be replaced by a dedicated computer. 'All the operations currently divided between batch and online systems will then be centred on a single online database. The intention is that duplication in the storage of records will have been largely eliminated, and it will be possible to search the MARC database as a single entity' (*The British Library Thirteenth Annual Report 1985–86*). This will have the added advantage of significantly reducing British Library's expenditure on mainframe computing.

BLAISE RECORDS, British Library's latest online service, initiated in 1987, aims to reduce on-site cataloguing costs by providing machine-readable bibliographical records at an economically acceptable rate from the world's largest MARC database. The entire array of British Library files–BNBMARC, Whitaker, H&SS, SRIS, DSC monograph file, the catalogue files of the Map and Music libraries, AVMARC and SIGLE will be supporting the new service. Should requests draw a blank from these files they will be recycled against the mighty North American OCLC Online Union Catalogue. 'BLAISE RECORDS–a New MARC Record Service', *BS Newsletter*, No. 43, June 1987:7 gave advance information whilst *BLAISE RECORDS Don't Stand Alone!*, an A4 folded wallet contains a number of factsheets on the new service: the databases, how to become a user (equipment needed and subscription procedures); costs; BLAISE RECORDER software; and a promotional brochure. The full significance of BLAISE RECORDS in the context of British Library's awareness of changing library needs emerges from Robert Smith's 'MARC record supply: the British Library reacts to a changing environment', *Library Association Record*, **89**, (9), September 1987:466 and in 'BLAISE RECORDS News', *BS Newsletter*, No. 44, October 1987:6. BLAISE RECORDER software is claimed to make MARC record acquisition an effortless task and features a search creation facility with ISBN validation; an auto-log in facility; a stored search recycling programme; and a downloading facility.

Ephemeral and permanent documentation promotes and supports all the BLAISE Services. A series of uniform A4 folded leaflets, including separate price lists, provide concise information on all aspects of the services currently available. *Cataloguing Services. How BLAISE Cataloguing Services Can Help You* advises subscribers on the local data processing capabilities of two magnetic tape services, Exchange Tapes and the Selective Record Service, the one an economical method of purchasing complete sets of all MARC records, the other intended for organizations requiring individual records from the British Library database. *BLAISE Services. How To Use British Library Online Services Through Your Micro* briefs potential users on what facilities are necessary to access BLAISE-LINE and BLAISE-LINK. For those hesitant or diffident of their capacity to comprehend technical terminology, the basic requirements listed and the detailed inventory of points to look for when selecting or writing software, upgrade this leaflet to the absolutely indispensable class. Almost in the same category is *BLAISE-LINE. Your questions answered*, inserted in *Library Association Record*, **87**, (4), April 1985, distributed to explain the facts about BLAISE-LINE and to sing its praises to reference librarians. *BLAISE-LINE Helping People Get Things Done*, now replacing *BLAISE-LINE Your Window On Knowledge*, indicates the databases accessed, emphasizes its commanding role in the information chain, and describes the bibliographical information it provides. Procedures for sample searches are outlined.

BLAISE-LINE Workbook is designed to help new users to obtain a good working knowledge of the system. 'Novice searchers are guided through basic steps such as logging on and entering a simple search. The *Workbook* also helps users to learn more complex ways of searching the system, and is useful for newcomers to BLAISE-LINE, whatever their existing level of online expertise.' *BLAISE-LINE Mini Manual* (3rd edition, 1985), for use at the terminal, 'is intended both as an introduction to various technologies and as a quick reference guide to individual files when searching online'. Accordingly, part one provides instruction on how to log on and off, how to select records for output to tape, and how to carry out a subject search. Part two describes 11 databases currently available with details of coverage, file data, access, sample records and search terms. A list of common errors made by users when logging in or searching, together with possible explanations, is appended. *BLAISE-LINE User Manual*, published in two substantial ring binders to allow for the ready insertion of updating fascicules, is a detailed guide to the BLAISE-LINE system. Early sections describe the retrieval facilities available whilst later sections examine each of the files which can be searched. A BLAISE-LINE glossary is included.

BLAISE-LINK. How BLAISE-LINK Can Help You, an A4 folded leaflet, emphasizes its immense bibliographic resources, on instant access, for literature subject searches, for compiling lists of items by known authors, for collecting data on chemicals, and for tracing details of journal articles. Its ease of search, its reliability, its value for money, its ease of access are also stressed. A descriptive list of 20 specialist BLAISE-LINK databases is inserted. *INTROMED. A Workbook For use With The Medline Training File On BLAISE-LINK* is an easy introduction to online searching on MEDLINE. Units on how to log on and to enter a simple search and print the results are followed by information on more complex searching strategies. A terminal exercise on INTROMED, a special BLAISE-LINK training file, is included along with multiple-choice paper exercises to check understanding of the points covered. An 18-page BLAISE-LINK glossary brings comfort to users unfamiliar with online information retrieval terminology. *The BLAISE-LINK Mini Manual* (3e, 1985) is an introduction for new users and a quick reference guide when searching online. Instructions are given on logging in and off, error correction, BLAISE-LINK commands, searching, stringsearching, Offsearch, Savesearch and Storesearch, and printing. *The BLAISE-LINK User Manual* is more detailed: early sections describe the retrieval facilities, instructions on logging in, searching, printing, offsearch, storesearch; later sections look at the files available. All subscribers receive updated sheets.

BLAISE Services Newsletter, circulated monthly to BLAISE subscribers, was first issued under its former title *BLAISE Newsletter* in June 1977. It is very much intended for operational use and contains technical information and reports on developments in the MARC format. Matters raised at users' meetings are featured and contributions and feedback from readers are welcomed. Its present title was assumed with issue number 76, September/October 1985. The first issue presented a perspective of BLAISE services just three months after their commencement. Another early survey was Brian Collinge's 'BLAISE', *Aslib Proceedings*, **30**, (11–12), October–November 1978:394–402 which covered the whole range of BLAISE services as they stood at the time. More recent progress reviews are David Butcher's 'BLAISEing the trail: developments at the British Library Services Division', *Refer*, **3**, (2), Autumn 1984:1–4 and 'Ten Years Of BLAISE Online Services', *BS Newsletter*, No. 43, June 1987:1–3 which also ventures a look at the future. Susan Hill contributes some personal memories in 'The Early Days' printed in *10 Years Of BLAISE Online*, a special supplement to *BLAISE Services Newsletter*, No. 38, September/October 1987.

Bibliographic Services Division Newsletter was first issued in May 1976 to present information about the Division's policies, activities, and services. A change of title to *Bibliographic Services Newsletter* was effected from February 1986. An overview of BSD complete with an organizational chart illustrating the range of its activities, with sections on the development of PRECIS, CIP, the UK Serials Data Centre and the international MARC network, appeared in the first issue. A similar state of the art presentation, revised at intervals, would be a welcome feature in all the Divisional newsletters.

Bibliographic Services has not attracted the same volume of documentary coverage as other British Library Divisions. Richard E. Coward's 'The British Library Bibliographic Services Division', chapter 7, *British Librarianship Today* (Library Association, 1976) is valuable for the early years whilst A. E. Jeffrey's 'Bibliographic Services Division', *Library Review*, 32, Spring 1983:67–77 condenses an impressive amount of information into a relatively short space. Andy Stephen's 'The Bibliographic Control of Publishing in the United Kingdom', *British Book News*, May 1987:256–7 examines British Library's function as the national bibliographic agency. Its continuing story may be conveniently followed in successive issues of British Library's *Annual Report*.

Part 3

Science, Technology and Industry

Document Supply Centre

Central Library for Students–National Central Library + DSIR Lending Library Unit–National Lending Library for Science and Technology=British Library Lending Division–Document Supply Centre

The Central Library for Students (CLS) came into existence 1 March 1916 to supply books needed by adult classes run by the Workers' Education Association, founded 13 years earlier, and quickly became engaged in lending public libraries copies of books required by their readers but not otherwise available. Its progress towards becoming the recognized centre for interlibrary lending within the United Kingdom, was foreshadowed and accelerated by the Report of the Public Libraries Committee (the Kenyon Report) of 1927 which stated that 'the solution of the problems of making the resources of the libraries of government departments, of universities and of special libraries of every kind, more accessible to the general public lies in the development of the Central Library for Students as a bureau of exchange for all libraries'. The *Report* recommended that the CLS should be reconstituted as a special department of the British Museum, gaining both specialized bibliographical expertise and prestige which would command public confidence. If this close relationship with the British Museum had been effected the CLS would have entered the British Library by a different route but the Museum's trustees foresaw difficulties in becoming involved in CLS's direct management, preferring to indicate their support by nominating some of their number to the Board of the new library.

The *Report's* proposals were referred to the Royal Commission on National Museums and Galleries which recommended

Treasury funding of £3,000 per annum to transform the CLS into a National Central Library (NCL). A Royal Charter, granted 21 April 1931, defined NCL's objects: 'to supply on loan to libraries, or in exceptional cases to individuals books for study which cannot conveniently be obtained in any other way; to supply such books on loan to groups of adult students; to act as an exchange or clearing house for mutual loans of such books between other libraries; to act as a centre of bibliographical information, both for national and international purposes; and to facilitate access to books and information about books', an amalgam of its original and recommended new responsibilities. NCL's subsequent history to its enforced and reluctant merger with the National Lending Library of Science and Technology to form the British Library Lending Division in 1973, and the development of the national interlibrary lending system, is chronicled in S. P. L. Filon's *The National Central Library. An experiment in library co-operation* (Library Association, 1977). D. J. Urquhart's 'The National Central Library—A Historical Review', *Journal of Documentation*, **34**, (3), September 1978:230–9 is an argumentative critique. Filon's 'The National Central Library', *Library World*, **LXII**, (727), January 1961:153–7 presents an inside view of its management and functional structure.

The *fons et origo* of the National Lending Library for Science and Technology (NLLST) may be perceived in an unpublished 1949 report by the Committee on Industrial Productivity's Panel on Technical Information Services which noted that 'the development of technical library facilities has failed to keep pace with the growth of scientific research'. Much public money was being invested in scientific research but comparatively little on scientific library and information services. To offset this imbalance the Panel recommended the establishment of a Scientific and Technical Library Authority charged with setting up a national lending library, not necessarily based in London, and a centralized reference collection which should be in the capital. In 1950 the Panel's responsibilities were transferred to the Advisory Council for Scientific Policy whose Standing Scientific and Technical Information Committee recommended a new national scientific lending library outside London, preferably in the industrial North and Midlands, for which it might also serve as a scientific reference library, to be administered by the Department of Scientific and

Industrial Research (DSIR).

Active planning started on a new national library designed to provide a postal loans service for scientific and technical literature within the United Kingdom in November 1956. When Dr D. J. Urquhart, a member of the former Panel on Technical Information Services, was put in charge of what became known as the DSIR Lending Library Unit, his first task was to build up the new library's collections. Current scientific and technical literature began to be purchased with priority given to Russian scientific literature because of the clear inadequacy of existing collections of this type of material. Selection of periodicals was initially based on the current holdings of the Science Museum Library (SML) and on systematic scrutiny of national lists and bibliographies. A survey of the use of the SML's periodical collections was the basis for determining what initial back files would most likely be needed. Much of the SML's periodical holdings had been primarily acquired for loan purposes and these were transferred to the new library in bulk.

As the innovative nature of the new library unfolded it was soon apparent that it was to be a library run by scientists and not by librarians along traditional lines. 'The majority of the literature was to be shelved in alphabetical order of title, for this was the quickest and most economic way to deal with requests in a postal loan as opposed to a reference service. Records were to be kept to a minimum and there was to be no library catalogue, at least in the traditional form' (R. M. Bunn, 'How It All Began', *BLL Review*, **2**, (3), July 1974:75–8). Published abstracts and bibliographies, where they existed, were to be used as guides to the Library's holdings–where they did not exist the library would prepare and publish its own bibliographic records. A former Royal Ordnance Factory at Thorpe Arch, near Boston Spa, in the West Riding of Yorkshire, was ultimately selected as the location of the new Library. Boston Spa could provide good postal communications via Leeds and the site afforded ample space for expansion. Work started in October 1959 to convert a number of storage buildings, and in 1961 current serial literature began to arrive, the first stage of an unprecedented large-scale move which was finally completed in July 1962. In total 300,000 volumes (or 600 tons) were transported in 140 rail containers to Boston Spa. Incredibly no item was unavailable for lending for more than 48 hours. NLLST was formally opened by the Minister for Science, November 1962. Its antecedents and early history are well-chronicled in Bernard Houghton's *Out Of The Dinosaurs. The Evolution Of The National Lending Library For Science And Technology* (Clive Bingley, 1972).

In six short years the DSIR Lending Library Unit had been transformed into a new national library with an initial stock of 300,000 volumes, with 12,000 current serials and nearly as many on order. But it was not only the speed with which NLSST had been created that impressed, although its planning had been in the hands of a small section within DSIR, comments and suggestions had been widely trawled while the plans were still fluid, notably in Urquhart's 'The National Lending Library For Science and Technology', *Journal of Documentation*, **13**, (1), March 1957:13–31. Considerable thought was given to the problems that would confront the Library: the uncertainty of the future world output of scientific literature and its effect on the NLLST's operations; how far photocopies and micro-publications could be utilized; and to what extent new techniques such as data processing could be pressed into service in meeting the anticipated demands on NLLST's resources. Bunn's 'Planning A National Lending Library For Science And Technology', *Aslib Proceedings*, **9**, (9), September 1957:280–8 gives an insight into DSIR's short-term and long-term planning exercises whilst Urquhart's 'The U.K. National Lending Library For Science And Technology', *Unesco Bulletin For Libraries*, **XIII**, (8–9), August–September 1959:173–5 represented a halfway look at some of the problems and exposes the author's new concept of interlibrary lending. How the Library set about its tasks, the methods it employed and the services it offered were vividly presented in a glossy, illustrated, 20-page brochure, *National Lending Library For Science & Technology*, first printed in March 1967.

When the Dainton Committee turned its attention to the national lending services it recognized that the NLLST had very rapidly become 'a highly successful means of satisfying loan and photocopying requests for scientific material' (Dainton *Report*, para. 236). In significant contrast, 'requests for loans in the humanities and the social sciences are less frequently satisfied than requests for scientific material handled by the NLLST. In addition, inter-library lending arranged through the NCL is all too often slow...' (para 254). 'Consideration of all the relevant factors' led to one inescapable conclusion: 'an early transfer of the NCL's loan stocks to Boston Spa' (para 259). The Government White Paper which followed agreed: to provide 'an efficient central lending and photocopying service in support of the other libraries and information systems of the country' it would be necessary 'to expand the lending facilities at Boston Spa in Yorkshire in order that all the lending activities of the British Library may be concentrated there'. And so, after 57 years, the separate existence of the NCL came to an end; 750,000 volumes were transported from London to Yorkshire, an operation that dwarfed even the original move 11 years earlier, graphically described in 'The Transfer Of The National Central Library To Boston Spa', *BLL Review,* **2**, (1), January 1974:5–11. The British Library Lending Division was formed 1 July 1973. Its progress since then, until it was redesignated Document Supply Centre (DSC) in the 1985 restructure, can be followed in the July issues of *BLL Review, Interlending Review* and *Interlending and Document Supply.* Summary articles include Alan Day's 'Lending Division', *Library Review,* 32, Spring 1983:45–63 and K. P. Barr's authoritative and well-documented 'The British Library Lending Division: The First Ten years', *Interlending and Document Supply,* **11**, (3), July 1983:79–91.

DSC is the largest library in the world devoted to interlibrary loans. It systematically collects and supplies all manner of documents to supplement the collections of other libraries within the United Kingdom by lending and making photocopies of its own stock whenever possible. Approximately 88 per cent of all requests are satisfied in this way. Arrangements are made with various other libraries possessing large and relatively unexploited specialized collections, including copyright libraries, to act as 'back-up' libraries which lend or photocopy items on request to satisfy demands which cannot be satisfied from DSC's own resources. Serials Copying Units operate in Humanities and Social Sciences and in the Newspaper Library at Colindale. Its current acquisition programme embraces an extensive selection of serial publications in most languages from all parts of the world. All significant English language monographs wherever published are acquired but material at a lower level is not purchased. Reports, translations and theses are acquired by special arrangements whilst a special effort is made to acquire conference proceedings. Official publications of the United Kingdom and of major intergovernmental organizations are acquired; those of other countries are bought only on demand. Music scores, too, are within DSC's sphere of acquisition but not popular sheet music or orchestral and vocal sets. Only a selection of foreign language monographs is acquired although Russian scientific literature continues to be systematically collected.

To cope with the volume of requests (3,150,000 in 1986/87) DSC's systems and procedures remain geared to processing them as fast as possible, and most are turned round within 48 hours. Its current book catalogue is now available on BLAISE-LINE, allowing libraries to use their own terminals and microcomputers to streamline interloan procedures by putting their requests through BLAISE-LINE's online document request service ORDER. An Urgent Action Service was first introduced for UK users on an experimental basis in May 1982. Telephone requests are dealt with by a special team who aim to reply within two hours and send off whatever document is required the same day. For very urgent requests photocopies of articles can be despatched within hours by Facsimile transmission (FAX). A similar service was inaugurated for European users in December 1983 and later extended overseas. More details are included in *Urgent Action Service Users' Guide* and *International Services Urgent Action on Fax*, two A5 leaflets, and in 'Spotlight on our U.K. Urgent Action Service', *BLLD Newsletter*, No. 2, June 1985:3.

For users who process their requests through microcomputers or communicating word processors an Automated Request Transmission by Telephone (ARTTel) service is available. A twice-folded A4 leaflet, *ARTTel Technical Instructions (UK)* provides notes on hours of availability and equipment required and instructions on operating procedures. Lists of requests, either in the form of typed lists, computer printouts, abstract citations or any other form of listing can be accepted by post, telex or FAX for processing by a special staff team. *Users' Handbook UK* (5e, 1987) endeavours to ensure that borrowing libraries correctly follow set procedures to facilitate the fastest possible service. A simplified guide to DSC's internal procedures, how to complete postal request forms, information on the Automated Request Transmission services, the type of material held and not held, enquiries information and notes on DSC's other services and the transport schemes, are all included. A *Directory of Library Codes* enables users to convert locations given in code form into the names and addresses, telex and telephone numbers of libraries which may be able to supply items not held at DSC.

Document Supply Centre. A brief guide, a vivid three-coloured A5 folded leaflet, introduces its resources, acquisition programme, systems and procedures, and means of access. In the light of DSC's relatively isolated location *Services For Visitors And Arrangements For Visits*, an A5 twice-folded, semi-stiff, vertically opening leaflet, is doubly useful, containing notes on the types of material covered in its acquisition policy, on reading room services, online searches, tours, restaurant and banking facilities, travel and accommodation advice and information, and a diagrammatic map. More detailed travel information for those arriving by train, air, car or bus, is available on an A5 leaflet, *Travelling To The Document Supply Centre*. Once at Boston Spa another A5 folded leaflet, *Reading Room Service*, explains how easily any item in DSC's stock of 2½ million books, 180,000 serial titles or 3 million microforms can be consulted. Advice is given that a personal visit can be useful to scan a wide range of documents, to consult a long run of journal issues, or to search abstracts and indexes not readily accessible elsewhere.

A 12-minute video, *The British Library Document Supply Centre at Boston Spa*, is available in VHS (PAL, NTSC and SECAM) standards. Gavin Holman's *Automation At The British Library Document Supply Centre* (1987) describes the current state of all automation activities at Boston Spa and is intended for use by British Library staff, and by visitors who are obviously expected to have a sound grasp of technical detail. Those arriving in organized parties may also be handed an internally-produced document, *Systems And Procedures At Boston Spa*, updated at regular intervals, which proceeds at descriptive pace through all sections of DSC with a number of illuminating flowcharts. Three glossy illustrated brochures contain some striking interior and exterior photographs. The first two, *The Urquhart Building* and *Extensions to the Urquhart Building* are both now unfortunately out of print. The third, *25 Years of document supply from Boston Spa*, traces DSC's short history and includes some wickedly chosen before-and-after quotations. 'Our 25th birthday', *DSC Newsletter*, No. 8, September 1986:1 also takes a brief look back. *Facts & Figures*, a widely-distributed A4 folded leaflet, dated April of each year, gives statistical information on all aspects of DSC's operations: stock, record creation, its users, demand, prices, computer search services, gifts and exchanges, staff, costs, and buildings and equipment, a complete overview in figures.

Formerly known as MEDLARS (Medical Literature Analysis and Retrieval System), the Medical Information Service provides expert computer literature searches, either a current awareness service or retrospective searching of more than 80 databases, including MEDLINE, EXCERPTA MEDICA, BIOSIS, and TOXLINE, through BLAISE-LINK, DATASTAR and DIALOG. Direct online access to BLAISE-LINK is available for libraries and information units enjoying their own terminals. A complete literature back-up is also offered, every item quoted can be supplied through DSC's lending services. Four current topic bibliographies are published: *Complementary Medicine Index* (monthly); *Occupational Therapy Index* (monthly); *Physiotherapy Index* (monthly), and *Sports Medicine Index* (bimonthly). Citations are arranged in broad subject groupings and each issue includes full author and subject keyword indexes. *Computer Searches*, an A4 information booklet, takes the form of a semi-stiff folder carrying details of database searches in medicine, health care, pharmacology, and toxicology, together with information on the types of search available, examples of print format, and charges. The folder encloses various informative leaflets.

DSC's Gift and Exchange Service (GES), reformed in 1974 from the NCL's British National Book Centre and NLLST's Disposal Section, continues to operate within the UK although its international service was suspended at the end of 1981. GES's purpose is to assist libraries to dispose of no-longer wanted items either by receiving them into DSC's own stock to ensure that at least one copy survives for loan, or else by offering them to other libraries by means of regularly circulated lists available by subscription. The Service is featured in 'It's a gift', *BLLD Newsletter*, No. 4, December 1985:2. A Northern Listening Service for Recorded Sound in the reading room at Boston Spa, inaugurated in May 1985, allows access by appointment to virtually any item held by the National Sound Archive. Full details regarding enquiries, appointments and the type of material available are printed in an A5 folded leaflet, *Northern Listening Service For Recorded Sound*.

NLLST's policy of preparing and publishing its own

bibliographic records of its holdings still continues. SJE's 'The British Library Lending Division's Bibliographic Publications', *Interlending Review*, **10**, (2), April 1982:62–3 describes them as 'essentially finding lists, in many cases developed originally to facilitate internal access to documents and published subsequently because of their general utility'. *Current Serials Received*, first published at irregular intervals, but annually since 1978, now lists all titles received by DSC and SRIS with corresponding shelfmarks. It is divided into three alphabetical sections: titles in Roman script; transliterated titles from Cyrillic script; and cover-to-cover translations of Cyrillic script serials. Journals are entered under their current titles although many holdings include back files under earlier titles. *Keyword Index To Serial Titles* (KIST) is a keyword listing of all current and retrospective holdings of DSC (192,000 titles), SRIS (64,000), Science Museum Library (10,000) and Cambridge University Library (77,000). The 1987 edition also lists frequently requested Humanities and Social Sciences serials (11,000) and some selected titles held by the Newspaper Library. Plans are afoot to input the holdings of other libraries. Subscribers receive a set of fiche with an introductory guide in January and replacement sets every quarter.

Index Of Conference Proceedings Received, published monthly, covers all types of conference proceedings and symposia. It indexes over 200,000 conferences in all disciplines with some 18,000 added each year. Use is by subject keyterms taken from the conference title, with entries in the language of the proceedings, but with English terms being preferred for multilingual conferences. Information is provided on the date, venue, conference title, sponsoring body and DSC's shelfmark. Annual cumulations since 1974 are complemented by *BLL Conference Index 1964–1973* and a quinquennial volume 1974–1978. In addition *Index of Conference Proceedings Received 1964–1981* provides access on microfiche to over 146,000 conference proceedings. The *Index* is available online through the Conference Proceedings Index service. By virtue of DSC's comprehensive collection of published proceedings the *Index* is indispensable for tracing this notoriously awkward category of material.

British Reports, Translations and Theses (BRTT) lists report literature and translations produced by British government organizations, industry, university and other learned institutions, as well as selected official publications not published by HMSO and local government documents. It also includes most doctoral theses accepted at British universities and reports and 'unpublished' translations from the Republic of Ireland. Published monthly, with microfiche quarterly and annual indexes, *BRTT* is arranged in three major sections: Humanities, Psychology and Social Sciences; Biological and Medical Sciences; and Mechanical, Industrial, Civil and Marine Engineering. 'Spotlight on BRTT', *DSC Newsletter*, No. 6, June 1986:3 gives an insight into its compilation. The reports in *BRTT* form part of DSC's input to the System for Information on Grey Literature in Europe (SIGLE) database which has been publicly available on BLAISE-LINE since August 1984.

Books At Boston Spa, a microfiche catalogue produced six times a year, first made available in 1987, lists in one alphabetical sequence all English Language and Western European language books published from 1980 onwards held by DSC. An introductory guide is supplied with the original set of fiche and subscribers receive fully cumulated replacement sets at two-monthly intervals. *Current British Journals* (4e, 1986), a subject guide to periodicals published in association with the UK Serials Group, contains some 7,500 titles of UK journals arranged by subject on a broad UDC basis. The intention is to issue a revised version every two years. Information includes titles; date of first publication; previous title(s); publishers' name, address and telephone number; indication of subject content; availability of indexes; circulation figures, and the existence of microform editions.

Journals In Translation (4e, 1987), published jointly with the International Translations Centre in Delft, lists over 100 titles from all subject areas, either translated cover-to-cover, or selectively, together with journals consisting of article translations collected from multiple sources. An original title index, a keyword-in-context subject index, and a list of publishers and distributing agents are also included. Since 1959 the Library has sponsored cover-to-cover translations of a number of Russian scientific and technical journals. DSC is responsible for the financial control of the programme but the translating and technical editing, production and marketing, are in the hands of various research associations, learned societies, and, in one instance, of a commercial publisher. Titles, frequency, contents and prices are listed in a 210mm × 100mm folded leaflet, *Translated Research Journals*.

Current Research in Britain, an annual register of UK research succeeds the three-volumed *Scientific Research in British Universities, Polytechnics and Colleges* published by BSD 1979 to 1981 when it was transferred to BLLD. It is now published in four volumes: *Physical Sciences; Biological Sciences; Social Sciences,* and *The Humanities.* Each entry comprises researchers' names, a description of the project, its sponsoring body and the dates of the project. There is a name index listing all researchers with references to their projects, a study area index accessed by specific keywords, a keyword index and a department index. The latest edition contains details of 65,000 projects, 18,000 of them for the first time. *Current Research* is available online through Pergamon Infoline.

DSC has always produced its own journals: *NLL Review* started in 1971 changing title to *BLL Review* when BLLD was formed two years later. *BLL Review* was first seen as a quarterly house journal disseminating news and information about BLLD's activities but a change of emphasis came in 1975, when it was decided that in order to promote debate in areas in which BLLD was closely concerned, the *Review* should carry not only reports of surveys, research and other activities, but also relevant papers from extramural contributors on general topics regarding interlibrary cooperation, the availability and bibliographic control of particular types of literature, the storage and handling of library stock, etc. So marked did this change of direction become that a further change of title to *Interlending Review. Journal Of The British Library Lending Division* was considered necessary in 1978. The present title, *Interlending and Document Supply,* was assumed in 1983 and the journal now aims to cover 'the supply of documents between organizations, by lending and other means, in developed and developing countries; reports of research on document supply; acquisition, storage and photoduplication of stock; regular reviews and bibliographies of recent literature on document supply; and information on relevant new publications'. A new quarterly review, *Science and Technology Policy,* is announced for 1988 to succeed *The Social And Economic Impact of New Technology* formerly published by Technical Communications Ltd.

Because *Interlending and Document Supply* was available only on subscription, and not reaching as wide an audience as it might, and because its domestic Boston Spa coverage was diminishing, a quarterly *Newsletter* was launched in March 1985. Besides general information *DSC Newsletter*, now distributed five times a year, covers new developments, new services, links with other organizations, the use of new technology, staff changes and other matters judged to be of interest to users. A new design and a change of title to *Document Supply News* took effect from issue no. 14, December 1987. Until 1985 BLLD's Annual Report appeared in the July issue of the journal but has subsequently appeared in a special July issue of the *Newsletter*.

Science Reference and Information Service

Patent Office Library – National Reference Library of Science and Invention – Science Reference Library – Science Reference and Information Service

Created in 1852 to implement the Patent Law Amendment Act, the Patent Office was charged with the responsibility of regulating the granting of patents for invention covering new methods of manufacture. By disseminating patent information (the Patent Office immediately embarked upon a retrospective publication programme of patent specifications and drawings) industrial progress was stimulated and quickened whilst research and inventive power were suitably rewarded. A public scientific and technical library would provide an added stimulus to industrial and manufacturing development and the Library of the Great Seal Patent Office (POL) opened 5 March 1855 with a statutory obligation to provide public access to copies of all patents granted. By 1900 it had grown into a general scientific collection of 100,000 books but, after this initial spurt, the early years of the present century, especially the inter-war period, witnessed a decline in standards as successive governments resolutely refused to make the necessary resources available to build up the collections despite repeated recommendations to the contrary from professional and scientific societies.

At length, in 1951, the Scientific and Technical Information Committee proposed that the POL should be developed as the National Reference Library of Science and Invention (NRLSI). Nine years passed before the Lord Privy Seal and Minister of Science announced that the NRLSI would be constituted as part of the British Museum LIbrary, although housed as a separate unit, 'in the long term interest of learning, and of the completeness of

111

the national collections of scientific literature', and a further six years before this long-heralded, administrative rearrangement occurred in April 1966.

The Dainton Committee judged the NRLSI's future development would have no more in common with the BML than other units within a new national libraries organization and recommended that it should be transformed into a separate Central Science and Patent Collections but, in the event, this recommendation did not find favour with the Government. When the British Library was formed NRLSI became the Science Reference Library (SRL), one of four Departments comprising British Library Reference Division. It was redesignated Science Reference and Information Service (SRIS) in the 1985 reorganization, forming the Science Technology and Industry Division along with Document Supply Centre. Unlike Humanities and Social Sciences, British Library's other London-based reference collection, it is a library of first resort whose prime purpose is to serve librarians, information officers, technical journalists, abstractors, market researchers, translators and patent and trademark agents. At the moment there are two public reading rooms in West Central London, at 25 Southampton Buildings, Holborn for the inventive sciences, engineering, industrial technologies and business; and at 9 Kean Street, Drury Lane, Aldwych, a short walk away for life sciences, medicine, biotechnology, earth sciences, astronomy and pure mathematics. Both collections are freely available without formality but some delay may be experienced for older material stored in outhouses.

SRIS's history is reasonably well-documented although a comprehensive monograph is lacking. F. V. Gravell's 'The Patent Office Library', *London Librarian*, **5**, (5), May 1959:3, 5, 7–8 is an introduction to its history, services, stock and usage whilst his chapter with the same title in *The Libraries Of London* edited by Raymond Irwin and Ronald Staveley, (Library Association, 2re 1964), is a more extended account. Four papers printed under the title of 'National Reference Library Of Science And Invention', *Journal of Documentation,* **17**, (1), March 1961:1–39 are illuminating. R. S. Hutton charts the POL's decline from 1914 onwards, draws some unfavourable comparisons with the growth of similar collections overseas, emphasizes the significant increase in supply and cost of scientific literature, and reminds those in authority what exactly is involved in providing a national reference library service in science and technology. E. M. Nicholson has stringent observations on the resources allocated to the POL at a time when overlapping specialisms had 'transformed the problem of comprehensive provision for scientific and technological library needs into something of a new order of magnitude'. Maysie Webb reviews the POL's current activities, services and pattern of usage, speculates on what needs to be done during the changeover period, and anticipates the services the NRLSI will provide. A. H. Chaplin presents the BML point of view, outlining what its current acquisitions, especially of Slavonic and Eastern European material, will bring to the new library.

Maysie Webb's 'The National Reference Library Of Science And Invention: A Review Of Progress', *Journal of Documentation*, **22**, (1), March 1966:1–12 is a salutary paper for those who might imagine that all that is required when an old-established library is saddled with extra responsibilities is a change of title. In turn the selection, acquisition and classification of thousands of new books and periodicals, the cataloguing and classification processes involved, and the mechanics of working in close cooperation with BML staff, are all revealed in close detail. The broad principles of planning the new building are also disclosed. Susan Birds' 'The Science Reference Library', *State Librarian*, **24**, (2), July 1976:20–1 reports on its activities and services. M. W. Hill's 'The Science Reference Library', pp.73–83, *British Librarianship Today* (1976) sketches its history, looks at its accommodation difficulties especially in relation to stock location, remarks on its diverse clientele, and, by way of outlining the nature of its stock and services, illustrates the various roles the Library is required to fill: as a research library of last resort, and as a premier reference library of first resort in the field of science, technology and industry where 'it is a focal point in the network of information centres and services which cover the UK and a link with corresponding points abroad'. The same writer's 'From reference library to information service: a review of the changing role of the Science Reference and Information Service', pp.101–18, *The World of Books and Information* (The British Library, 1987), deals with the period 1967–85, *i.e.* from the time the Dainton Committee visited the NRLSI to its emergence in its latest SRIS plumage. SRIS's future is seen as being dependent on 'the extent to which it can continue to be a worthwhile and credible component of the information scene'. No doubt that applies to other divisions within the British Library conglomerate.

Janice Anderson's 'Science Reference Library', *The British Library. The Reference Division Collections* (1983) is an illustrated outline of its early history, collections and services, for the general reader whilst *Brief chronology of the British Library Science Technology and Industry division and its predecessors*, an A4 sepia leaflet, elucidates the complex institutional history, 1852–1986, of the libraries which now form the two arms of Science Technology and Industry division. Introductory information may be found on two widely distributed promotional leaflets: *Science Reference and Information Service*, 98mm × 210mm, folded concertina fashion, presents its nature and purpose, services and resources and a street map of Aldwych and Holborn; and the *British Library Services For Science Technology And Industry*, A5 folded, which advises on SRIS and DSC services and relevant publications.

In 1979 SRL issued a consultative paper *Access to Patent Documents and Information* seeking the views of interested organizations and individuals on its patent documentation policy. Such a review was not entirely unconnected with the annual cost, then running at £¾ million, of providing sets of patent documents to libraries away from London which guaranteed public access, a venerable practice instituted in the last century. The paper was also timely in that developments in document access and information supply promised a more cost effective system. As a result of the opinions expressed a Patents Information Network was established: six large city libraries–Birmingham, Glasgow, Leeds, Liverpool, Manchester and Newcastle–were designated Provincial Patent Libraries to receive published patent applications from the European Patent Office and the W.I.P.O. under the Patent Cooperation Treaty in addition to all UK and USA patents. These Libraries will provide reference and photocopying facilities and qualified staff to assist readers. The Network also includes a second group of 20 libraries, known as Patent Information Centres, offering similar services but which do not receive the same comprehensive documentation as the 'Big Six'. *Patents Information Network*, an A4 leaflet, lists libraries in both categories. 'A Renewed Patents Information Network For The United Kingdom', *SRL News*, No. 21, October 1980:1–2 and 'The Patents Information Network', *ibid.*, No. 22, April 1981:3 report events. The first issue of *PIN*

Bulletin, published quarterly by SRIS and available free from any of the Patents libraries, was first distributed late in 1981. 'The bulletin will give examples of the information which can be culled from patents available through the network as well as providing information about the network's participants and the services they provide' ('PIN Bulletin', *British Library News*, No. 72, January/February 1982:1). Peter J. Robson's 'Document Supply In The United Kingdom: Patents', *Interlending & Document Supply*, **14**, (2), April 1986:40–4 describes PIN as 'more than a grouping of passive document repositories' and urges interlibrary loans librarians to exploit its full potential. After a gap in publication, the *Bulletin* reappeared as *Patents Information News*. Dated Winter 1987, the first issue printed a complete list of member libraries of the UK Patents Information Network. SRIS's photocopy service by which patents may be obtained from its collections, at while-you-wait counters, by post or by telecommunication, is outlined in *Photocopy Service*, a concertina leaflet. *Patents Online Search Service*, a folded leaflet, encourages enquirers to make use of computerized searches to retrieve the information they require either in the form of bibliographic citations, abstracts or full patent specifications.

Helena M. Barton's soft-covered, A4, 60-page *Industrial Property Literature: A Directory of Journals* (1981), originally compiled for use by library staff, proved so helpful in answering enquiries that, although restricted to SRL's holdings, it was decided to make it more widely available. Arranged alphabetically by country, with a final section on international organization publications, it is a guide to the frequency and contents of over 350 patent, trademark and design journals. D. C. Newton's *Trade Marks: A guide to the literature and directory of lists and trade names* (2e, 1988) 'lists sources of information on trademarks most likely to be useful to agents, searchers and designers as well as to librarians and information scientists' (Introduction). It is presented in three sections: general literature, official trademark publications and a Directory of trade name lists.

Brenda M. Rimmer's *Guide To Official Industrial Property Publications* (1985), based on SRIS's holdings, assembles in a uniform sequence information on historical and current legislation; specifications; the contents of official gazettes; the availability and coverage of patent indexes; the scope and presentation of published information on designs and trademarks; reports of legal judgements and decisions; and on early publications, in geographical chapters relating to countries or groups of countries which persistently grant 1000 patents or inventors certificates a year. Countries with a lower output are also included if they form part of a recognized geographical or industrial group. Two final chapters deal with international conventions and the DERWENT and INPADOC computer-based searching systems. The *Guide* is in a loose-leaf format to allow for the insertion of revised sheets. *Industrial property publications in SRL*, distributed in the Aids To Readers series, is an annotated guide to the official publications held by SRIS for patents, designs, trademarks and plant breeders' rights for the United Kingdom, and the patent publications held as a result of the European Patent Convention and the Patent Cooperation Treaty. There is a separate section on secondary services, computer databases, and on the *Patent Information And Documentation Handbook* published in three loose-leaf volumes by the World International Property Organization in 1982. An A4, 20-page *Guide To Searching European Patent Convention (EPC) And Patent Cooperation Treaty (PCT) Literature* (1986) is constructed in the form of a manual so that individual sections may be consulted as required. Four ways of searching are outlined, by the names of the inventor or applicant, by subject, or by application number.

SRIS's Business Information Service offers a free quick-reference information and referral service by specialist staff in respect of company, product and market information supported by a charged searching of business online databases. A Working Group on Business Information was set up by British Library in February 1980 'to consider what should be the role of the national library in the provision of business information over the country as a whole, and what improvements might be made to the British Library's existing services...'. The Group examined collection development within the British Library, and the development of its associated information services, the adequacy of provision by other libraries, the support British Library should afford other libraries, and its priorities for action. *Business Information. The Role Of The British Library*, published as an A5 pamphlet in 1981, recommended that first priority should be the establishment of a national referral service for businesses, ideally to be located within the SRL, operating with specialist staff, geared to serve businessmen as well as information intermediaries and firms without libraries or information units. The second priority was to identify gaps in the provision of business information sources nationally and to extend its collecting policies to fill them. Most urgent was the acquisition of market research, stockholder's and financial reports, published in the UK and overseas. Company card services, trade and professional directories, extensive coverage of house, trade and business journals, from Britain, its major trading partners, and from the European Communities, were also placed in the urgent category. All were regarded as SRL's responsibility. So, too, were classified telephone directories from overseas, statistics relating to manufacturing, and multinational company reports. Other priority tasks were the development of information services, publicity for British Library holdings, and the provision of a comprehensive current bibliographical listing of all market research reports.

A Business Online Search Service (BIS) was inaugurated in December 1985 to take advantage of an expanding number of databases, accessing not only bibliographies but also full-text and directory-type files. 'Some databases have no direct printed equivalent and thus the information they contain may also be accessed this way' ('The BIS Online Search Service', *SRIS News*, No. 39, June 1986:5). An enhanced service, specializing in market, company and product information, was introduced in October 1987 on a subscription basis. In addition to its substantial resource bank of printed material–Extel and McCarthy cards, company and stockbroker reports, 20,000 UK and international trade catalogues, 5,000 trade and business journals, etc.–the new service takes advantage of commercial online databases such as Datasolve, Datastar, Dialog, Finsbury Data Services, and Pergamon Infoline. An introductory offer of five hours research time lures potential subscribers who will be charged £400 for ten hours on a regular basis. Further detail is printed in 'The Business Information Service Of The British Library', *SRIS Newsletter*, No. 2, October 1987:1.

A glossy A4 booklet, first distributed in May 1987, *Business Information* is a brief guide to all SRIS's business information reference resources intended to assist enquirers to exploit the business stock to the full. After an introductory map of the location of business information literature on the lower ground floor of

117

the Holborn reading room, there follow notes on all types of business information sources: company information; product information; market information; journals, house journals and newspapers; statistics; stockbrokers' reports; abstracting and indexing services; the online database search service; selected publicly available sources of business information in the UK; with a final section on guides to the business literature held at SRIS. Care has obviously been taken to present the information as clearly as possible, to the businessman as well as the information specialist. A large number of the Aids to Readers series of A4 information sheets relate to trade and business literature. *Trade Literature at the Science Reference Library* is an outline of holdings; *Trade directories at the Science Reference Library* lists the principal guides to directories and their location at Holborn; *Business literature at the Science Reference Library* summarizes the different types of literature held; *Statistics and market research information* notes that literature in this area has now been brought together, and outlines the publications available, market research reports and periodicals, trade and business journals, bibliographical sources of market research reports, official statistics and their guides, business monitors and unofficial statistics. A list of other libraries in the London area with major statistical and market research collections is appended.

Abstracting and indexing services for the business user lists such services in two sections: one dealing with those covering the whole spectrum of industry and commerce or specific aspects of business information; the other with those catering for particular industries. *Companies Registration Office Publications* itemizes specific titles held on microfiche in the trade directories section in the Holborn reading room. Information on company searching, liquidations and winding up, is also included and there is a list of known fee-based company search services. *Business Information: Guides-To-The-Literature Held At The Science Reference Library* annotates the small number of general information guides claiming to cover either the whole business field or a substantial part of it. Some highly specialized bibliographies and guides not suitable for inclusion in other Aids To Readers also find a place. All titles are listed according to region or country covered. *Company information sources at the Science Reference Library* describes some of the most important publications arranged under five headings:

financial activity; products and services; relationships between companies; commercial links, and small and unregistered business operations.

Other Business Information Service titles include P. M. Dunning's, 34-page *Trade Literature In British Libraries* (1985) providing information gathered from a questionnaire on material held, opening hours, conditions of access, personal contacts and local cooperative links of 30 major libraries and the 50-page *Trade Directory Information In Journals* (6e, 1986) covering journals held by SRIS which regularly contain trade directory information. Over 250 entries, including title of journal, its frequency, geographic coverage and scope of information, are arranged by subject.

The purpose of SRIS's Japanese Information Service launched in 1985 is the coordination and promotion of all existing library sources of Japanese scientific, technical and commercial information. 'This new service has been introduced against the background of a growing realisation in the West that if competition with Japan is to be on even terms, we must be as effective in exploiting information from Japan as the Japanese have been in exploiting information from sources foreign to them' ('New Japanese Information Service', *British Library News*, No. 110, August 1985:2). Annual seminars or conferences held 1984–7 confirm the widespread interest. *Information From Japan: Science Technology & Industry* (1985), papers from one of those seminars edited by Shirley V. King, includes an overview of the information scene in Japan, with details of patents, reports, conferences, specialized information services and translations. A business information section lists market research reports, directories and trade journals. *Japanese Journals In English* (1985), edited by Betty Smith and Shirley V. King, lists over 1000 scientific, technical and commercial journals arranged in subject keyword order. *Japanese Business Publications In English: A Select Annotated List Of Recent Publications Held By The British Library* (2e, 1987), edited by Sheila Edwards and Karen Thompson, contains sections on directories, statistics, market information and industry surveys, trade and business journals, bibliographies and abstract journals, and suppliers of literature published in Japan. A Japanese Online Search Service is now in operation; a Japanese language terminal at SRIS provides access to various Tokyo databases.

For the last five years SRIS has been investigating information in biotechnology. A pilot information service, BIOTEL, was set up in 1983 to examine the potential of PRESTEL in providing information in this area. BIOTEL was absorbed into the European Biotechnology Information Project (Ebip), formed in 1984 with European Community financial support, to identify and to document information sources including databanks, organizations and published material; to assess information needs, especially those of recently established companies, and to establish a pilot European Community-wide information and referral service. 'European Biotechnology Information Project Launched', *SRL News*, No. 27, June 1983:2; 'Science Reference Library', *British Library News*, No. 96, April 1984:1–2, and 'Ebip–set to continue', *ibid.*, No. 105, March 1985:2 record progress including the publication of *Ebip News*. European Community funding ended in March 1987 but the project immediately re-emerged as the British Library Biotechnology Information Service (BIS), an integral part of SRIS's operations. In January 1988, in collaboration with BioCommerce Data Ltd, BIS launched *Biotech Knowledge Sources*, a monthly current awareness journal, providing a comprehensive information service to specific industries engaged in biotechnology and to the research sector, making full use of information collated from research and industrial sources throughout Europe. 'British Library Biotechnology Information Service', *SRIS Newsletter*, No. 4, April 1988, has details. First issued in March 1988 *Biotechnology Information News* will appear quarterly, replacing *Ebip News*.

SRIS's Online Search Centre provides worldwide search facilities in relevant areas. *Online Databases Available At SRIS*, a 20-page A4 booklet, describes 172 databases arranged in nine categories: life sciences; earth sciences; chemistry and chemical engineering; technology; patents; trademarks; business; Japanese information; and miscellaneous, each cost-annotated per minute and per reference on and offline. Information on how to obtain a search; telephone numbers to contact; written, Telex or Fax addresses; the details required for search topics; and computer connect-time costs are also provided. Notes on this service and its advantages are printed in 'Online Search Centre', *SRIS Newsletter*, No. 3, January 1988:1–2. In December 1986 BLAISE-LINE launched SRIS-LINE, the catalogue of SRIS, with instant access to 175,000 books and periodicals covering all aspects of science, technology, business and industrial property literature. 'SRIS LINE–a new database for BLAISE-LINE', *BSD Newsletter*, No. 41, October 1986:4 and *Your Window On Science Technology & Business*, an A5 folded leaflet, expand on its coverage, subject access, search procedures and advantages.

A Linguistic Aid Service to help readers gain an understanding of the contents of scientific and technical literature printed in unfamiliar languages is offered by SRIS. The reader spends up to half an hour with a member of library staff with a reading knowledge of the language in question, examining the text and scanning key words, so that together they may determine whether a full translation would be worthwhile. *Linguistic Aid Service*, a bright orange A5 leaflet, stresses that this service is *not* a full translation service in itself.

Access to SRIS's collections is aided by a number of reference tools. B. A. Alexander's 72-page *Abstracting And Indexing Periodicals In The Science Reference Library* (1985) includes 1880 numbered entries covering the whole range of subject literature within SRIS's orbit whilst his *Journals With Translations Held By The Science Reference Library* (1985) lists in alphabetical order 500 plus publications of particular journals or articles from multiple sources covering literature in all sciences and technologies. There is an index of original titles. Both publications include subject indexes for headings and SRIS classmarks. *Directories Held By The Science Reference And Information Service* (2e, 1986), generated from SRIS's own catalogue database, lists upwards of 2000 directories on open access. Peter M. Dunning's *House Journals Held By The Science Reference Library* (2e, 1985) lists the journals of 750 companies worldwide ranging from those perhaps containing just one technical article to glossy company magazines or relatively primitive staff newsletters. Entries include location of company, house journal title, frequency and subject coverage. *Introduction to the SRIS classification*, included in the Aids To Readers series, is a full descriptive outline of location marks and shelf-order of the classified catalogue and of SRIS's classification scheme.

SRIS publishes a revised and updated edition of *Guide To Government And Other Libraries* every two years. The current 28th edition (1988) contains over 650 entries arranged in a subject sequence based on its own classification scheme supplemented by an alphabetical index of institutions. Entries include title of institution, address, telephone number, its departments, staff contacts, hours of opening, publications and, where available, Prestel, Telecom Gold Electronic Mail, and facsimile numbers.

The first issue of *SRIS Newsletter* appeared in June 1987. It will be issued three or four times a year and replaces *SRIS News*, formerly *SRL News*, which began publication in September 1973.

Part 4

Research and Development Department

Office for Scientific and Technical Information (OSTI) – Research and Development Department

When the Department of Scientific Research was dismantled in April 1965 its research activities were transferred to the Science Branch of the Department of Education and Science where the Office for Scientific and Technical Information came into being. Its functions were 'to advise the Secretary of State...on the conduct of, and support for, UK activities in scientific and technical information over the whole field of the natural and social sciences and their related technologies' and, secondly 'to keep under review the present arrangements for meeting information needs and to take action to improve these arrangements'. In particular it was to stimulate and, where necessary, to conduct all forms of research that might influence the effectiveness of scientific communications: the classification, storage, retrieval and translation of information; and the operation of information services for scientists and technologists. The promotion and development of new documentation techniques, and the improvement of the presentation in scientific communications in primary publications, literature guides, and in the compilation of selected data for scientists and engineers, were also to fall within its sphere of operations.

Despite its name, the emphasis on science quickly faded, and OSTI soon broadened its activities to include libraries and librarianship especially in the field of automation; the Dainton Committee noted that 'it was by far the largest single source of external funds for library research' and that 'a substantial proportion of its funds is spent on investigation into computer applications and other forms of library mechanization'. Because OSTI 'more than any other body, has, by the size of its resources, the opportunity to direct and coordinate library research effort', its services needed to be integrated into the new national library service. OSTI was not mentioned in the White Paper presented to Parliament for the establishment of the British Library but it was announced late in 1973 that, following discussions with the Advisory Committee on Scientific and Technical Information, and the British Library organizing committee, it would be moved to the Library with effect from 1 April 1974. The principal reasons given for this transfer of responsibility were the need for strong links on a continuous basis between libraries and information services and library and information research, and the expected growth of research within the British Library. Should OSTI and British Library go their separate ways a serious overlap of effort would dissipate resources and lead to unnecessary rivalry and competition.

At first the functions of British Library Research and Development Department (R & D) remained very much the same as OSTI's: identifying priorities for research, stimulating and supporting research; and promoting the application of results. But some changes in approach inevitably occurred. R & D now 'promotes and supports research and development related to library and information operations in all subject fields and is directed to the benefit of the national library and information system as a whole. . . . Support is not confined to library-orientated topics but is intended to cover all aspects of information generation, transfer and use.' It has continued OSTI's policy of providing support for semi-permanent Centres holding a continuing interest in a particular research field, affording the library and information world with information, education and advice and consultancy services. After a period of expansion up to 1981 when such Centres disposed of more than a third of the Department's allocated budget, putting a disproportionate strain on funds for individual projects, a new and more flexible funding system was introduced. The Centres were encouraged to seek additional research funds from other sources whilst R & D guaranteed continuing funding at reduced levels, and also permitted the Centres to apply for specific awards along the same lines, and in competition with, individual proposals. It was hoped that these new arrangements would enable the Centres 'to continue to provide a nucleus of knowledge about research and techniques in various fields of library and information science and, in addition, to provide services of direct relevance to the needs of the profession' ('British Library-supported centres', *R & D Newsletter*, No. 25, December 1982:4).

In order to assess the viability and potential value of research proposals a refereeing procedure has been adopted. An Advisory Committee for the Research and Development Department and a number of consultative groups drawn from the library and information world have been set up to assist in formulating and assessing research proposals. From time to time priorities for research are announced: the latest are embodied in *Priorities for Research 1985–89*, an A4 leaflet, summarized in *Library Association Record*, 87, (7), July 1985:257 and *British Library News*, No. 107, May 1985:1. Three broad areas of concern have been identified: the application of information technology for library and information services; the implications of information being treated as a tradeable commodity; and the effects of economic and social constraints on services. High priority is given to work on the applications and implications of information technology; to industrial, business and commercial information research; to information storage and retrieval; and to the dissemination of research results. Medium priority goes to research into information handling in the humanities with emphasis on how new technologies can be used; to user education; to research into education, manpower and training for the profession; to public library research; and to the application of technology into the conservation and preservation of library materials. 'Over and above these priorities the Department will seek to maintain programmes of work in the areas of science and engineering information research, publications research, information services to the library and information profession, user studies, and development projects.' In addition to its heavy publication programme R & D disseminates research results by means of conferences, seminars and workshops. In April 1988 R & D launched Library and Information Briefings in association with the Library & Information Technology Centre. These briefings cover the legal and political environment of information with subscribers receiving regular packages of description, comment and analysis of significant developments together with reading lists. Neil McLean's *Open Systems In Interconnection* and A. Aksoy's *Value Added Network Services* were the first two titles issued. Other topics expected to be covered at an early date include desktop publishing, CD-ROM, the workings and infrastructure of the European communities, electronic publishing, SGML and mark-up languages, and OPACs. At the end of the subscription year LIBs will be updated in a bound volume which will feature a review of the year's major developments and an index.

Following the transfer of BNB to the British Library in 1974 the BNB Research Fund was set up to commemorate those libraries, professional and book trade associations, and other institutions which, as members of BNB's Council, had supported the national bibliography in its early years. At the time of the merger BNB Ltd had considerable funds at its disposal and it was agreed by the British Library Board that an initial sum of £10,000 should be allocated on an annual basis. The objects of the fund were 'to promote bibliographic activities and related research' and 'to provide a means by which the member organizations of the former BNB Council can make proposals for support of bibliographical activities and related research of special interest to them and which are not likely to fall within the British Library's own activities and programme'. The transfer of assets was completed by January 1975 and the fund began its work a year later.

Although the fund let it be known it would receive applications for research in almost any area, it specifically excluded the compilation of bibliographies and historical bibliographical research unless such proposals were relevant to current bibliographical needs. Two areas in which proposals would be positively welcomed were identified as 'the study of interfaces between publisher, bookseller and librarian, with particular reference to the introduction and exploitation of machine-assisted methods' and 'research into books and their use, with emphasis on use in school libraries'. In recent years the Committee's interest has tended to be confined to new technology as it affects the book world. Hugh Pinnock's 'BNB research Fund', *Bibliographic Services Division Newsletter*, No. 6, August 1977:1–2 and Peter Stockham's 'BNB Research Fund looks for ideas', *Library Association Record*, **81**, (7), July 1979:331 carry relevant detail.

British National Bibliography Research Fund Reports are made available either priced or free; titles sold by R & D are described in *Publications from the R & D Department*; others are listed in *British National Bibliography Research Fund*, an eight-page A5 pamphlet reissued in October 1987.

All R & D funded projects result in research reports and *A Complete List of OSTI and BL R & D Reports 1965. Report numbers 5001–5653* is published in pocket-size booklet format. Reports are linked numerically, each entry gives author(s), institution where research was based, date of publication, and pagination. There are author, institution and title indexes. All reports are available on microfiche, some also in their original form. In 1982 a new series of Library and Information Research Reports likely to appeal to library professionals and to a wider public was launched in a convenient A5 paperback format. 'LIR Reports pay particular attention to new technology designed to improve the ways in which libraries are run and information is retrieved, collated, catalogued and transmitted. Reports in similar subjects are given covers of the same colour.' *Library and Information Research Reports. A series from the British Library Research and Development Department*, an updated annotated list, is distributed in A5 pamphlet form.

An *OSTI Newsletter* appeared quarterly from September 1966 reporting on such matters as policy developments, the award of new grants, and final and occasional progress reports. Although never intended to be anything more than a disposable document it soon transpired that many users retained the *Newsletter*. Its circulation built up to nearly 3000 and it was eventually furnished with an annual index. The first issue of *Research and Development Newsletter* was dated September 1974. An editorial was introduced in issue No. 25, December 1982: 'In recent years, the circumstances in which the Department operates have changed significantly, and this and future editorials will set out to inform readers as frankly as possible about these changes, and their effect on our policy for the support of new research.' Cumulated indexes were distributed for every six issues. Because of severe staff shortages the publication of the *Newsletter* was allowed to lapse, to be replaced after a three-year gap by two new titles: *R & D Department Bulletin,* to appear twice a year and, from January 1987, *British Library R & D Department Monthly Newsletter,* intended to increase knowledge and awareness of R & D's activities, but with circulation limited to selected representatives of the Library and Information Science profession. Planned to appear twice-yearly R & D's *Research Bulletin* commenced publication with a Winter 1987 issue. It follows a similar pattern to the old *Newsletter* carrying details of R & D's publications and activities.

Publications from the R & D Department, an A5, 24-page booklet, the most recent issue of which is dated April 1987, is a series by series annotated list of R & D publications in print. Margaret Mann's *Complete list of reports published by the British Library R&D* (British Library Information Guide 9, 1988) lists reports in numerical order with full bibliographical details and a short abstract of each report. These general catalogues are supplemented by a number of special information leaflets. *Information for Industry* (January 1985) notes that 'in a period of recession, it is more important than ever before that the decision-makers in industry are made aware of the benefits to be gained by the efficient use of information resources'. With this in mind R & D has undertaken 'a programme of research which will coordinate previous work and, where a need has been identified, support further studies'. The overall aim and objectives of its industrial, business and commercial information programme, research in progress, and the contents of recent R & D publications, are all outlined. *Online Information Retrieval* (October 1985) describes current research sponsored by R & D in the development of special interfaces to help the inexperienced searcher; the training of librarians and information scientists in search techniques; the testing of more sophisticated retrieval methods; the economic and marketing aspects of online publishing; and the effects of introducing online searching upon organizations. It lists publications and software produced since 1980. *Manpower, education and training* (October 1986), describes R & D's current involvement in research into these three related issues, and details research in progress and publications produced.

CD-ROM And New Technology Reports (November 1986), gives an account of British Library's demonstrations over the past year of its first compact disc which holds 500,000 bibliographic records. Various new technology reports are described including Ann Clarke's *The British Library's compact disc experiment* (1986). *Microcomputers in Libraries and Information Services* (November 1986), records R & D's current research commitment to novel applications of microcomputers in information handling and presentation. A report on research in progress precedes an annotated list of R & D and other publications in this area. Notes on research in progress and on the information service at the National

Foundation for Educational Research in England and Wales, are included in *Information skills in schools* (December 1986). *Electronic publishing* gives details of R & D supported projects and describes Project Quartet, the centrepiece of R & D's research programme 1986–1989, which is exploring ways of improving the flow of information in the academic research community. A *Quartet Newsletter* is issued.

British Library Information Guides are guides, directories and manuals, not concerned with research, published as A5 paperbacks. First in the series was *Family Directory: information sources on the family* edited by Jeffrey Weeks (1986). J. Stephens' *Inventory Of Abstracting And Indexing Services Produced In The U.K.* (BLIG 2, 1986) replaces two previous reports of the same title, R & D Report No. 5420 (1976) and Library and Information Research Report No. 21 (1983). It brings together 430 abstracting and indexing services covering documentary material published as journals, printed lists, or in micro or machine-readable form. There are four indexes: broad and specific subject headings, an index of responsible authorities, and an index of database producers with the UK online databases they provide. Graham P. Cornish's *Archival Collections of Non-Book Materials: a listing and brief description of major national collections* (BLIG 3, 1986) updates Joyce Line's preliminary list, R & D Report No. 5330 published in 1977 when British Library's attitudes to non-book media were still being formulated. Materials covered are film and video, sound recordings, photographic and mixed media collections. 'Those collections which perceive a national archival function as part of their role have been included together with a few collections which might be expected to have such a function but do not' (Abstract). Entries give location, telephone contact and opening hours. Current acquisitions policies, facilities for storage and archival preservation are described. *British Library Information Guides*, an A5 folded leaflet, is an annotated list of titles currently available.

British Library Research Reviews are commissioned overviews of specific topics in library and information science duplicated rather than typeset in an A4 format. Some are priced, others are free. British Library Research Papers are reports of research projects and meetings sponsored by R & D. 'In an effort to publish these reports quickly they are reproduced in-house in A4 format in the form in which they are received from the authors.' Both

Reviews and Papers are described in *Publications from the R & D Department*.

Authoritative documentation on OSTI begins with H. T. Hookway's 'The Developing Role Of OSTI', *Library Association Record*, **69**, (10), October 1967:346–50 which emphasizes how far its functions have extended 'so that within the resources at its command it may stimulate or undertake almost any activity that can contribute to better handling or utilization of information in both the natural and social sciences and their related technologies'. J. C. Gray's 'Library Research And Innovation: the role of OSTI', *Libri*, **20**, (1–2), 1970:1–5 is a rapid policy survey. *OSTI The First Five Years. The Work of the Office for Scientific and Technical Information*, (HMSO, 1971), must be the starting point for any close examination of OSTI's role in research activity during its first quinquennium. It outlines the principal activities OSTI supported, within the broad framework of policy as it evolved, and examines how these activities influenced the work of scientists, technologists and information specialists. A list of OSTI grants is appended as is a list of reports and published work resulting from OSTI-supported research.

The transitional period is well covered in 'The Research and Development Department', pp.16–19, *The British Library Second Annual Report 1974–75* which identifies key areas of research and some priority projects. John C. Gray's 'The British Library Research and Development Department', *State Librarian*, **29**, (1), March 1981:2–3, 5 looks at R & D's background, its role in government coordination of information activity, what library research can achieve, and the dissemination of research results. The most comprehensive and critical account, encompassing its OSTI origins and legacy, its policies and projects, its costs, structure and staffing, its grant applications and refereeing system, the relation between R & D's policies and financial restraints, an assessment of its achievements, and some contemporary criticism, is undoubtedly Philip Whiteman's 'Research and Development Department', *Library Review*, 32, Spring 1983:81–109, generally applauded as the most scholarly and perceptive contribution to that journal's 'This Emphatically British Library The First Ten Years Of The British Library' special issue. Sir Peter Swinnerton-Dyer's 'The evolution of the British Library's research policy' in *The World Of Books And Information* (British Library, 1987) underlines R & D's inability to fund everything it would wish and traces the emergence of its list of research priorities. R & D's policies relating to the extent of financial aid it is prepared to consider, and its high and medium priorities, are outlined in Henry East's *A Guide To Sources Of Funds For Research And Development In Library And Information Science* published in the British Library Information Guide series in 1987.

Part 5

Story without end

Most Urgent Need

'A new building on the Bloomsbury site is the British Library's most urgent need' the *First Annual Report 1973–4* pronounced. The need had been apparent since 1859 when the Trustees of the British Museum had turned down a proposal to purchase an adjacent site on the grounds that the asking price of £445,000 was too high. Ninety years later, the same site of seven acres across the other side of Great Russell Street, immediately facing the front entrance of the British Museum, bounded by Bloomsbury Way and New Oxford Street to the south, by Bloomsbury Street on the west and Bloomsbury Square on the east, was designated under the Town and Country Planning Act of 1947 as the site for a new Library. In 1964 the Government and Trustees accepted the architect's plans and the local authority, Holborn Borough Council, agreed to cooperate on condition that the rebuilding would include as much residential and commercial development as could be reconciled with the construction of a new library complex.

And then, without ever really appreciating they were in a battle, the Trustees lost a war. The Labour Government of the day announced in 1967 that objections by the London Borough of Camden, successors to Holborn Borough Council, would be upheld. The political uproar which followed was instrumental in the appointment of the Dainton Committee who reported that much of the evidence it received concerned the future site of a new building to replace the BML, a strong body of opinion urging that the Museum's library departments should be kept close to the antiquities departments in Bloomsbury, a view that endured to bedevil the issue of a new building, and one which opponents to the site at St Pancras are still exploiting. No hard and fast conclusions emerged from the Committee's deliberations on this

137

issue although it was convinced that 'from library considerations alone...the Bloomsbury site is the most suitable for the National Reference Library'. If not at Bloomsbury then certainly in Central London. The Government accepted the Dainton Committee's recommendation, as did the incoming (June 1970) Conservative Government whose White Paper to Parliament remarked that both the BML and the NRLSI were bursting at the seams and desperately needed rehousing. 'The site for their new buildings will be in the seven acres lying between New Oxford Street and Great Russell Street, and immediately adjacent to the British Museum.'

The Government was satisfied that the Bloomsbury site could accommodate the new Reference Division *in toto*, including the Science Reference Library, whilst at the same time preserving all the important listed buildings and incorporating as much housing as earlier plans had envisaged. Two years of planning ensued and moves were put in hand to acquire those parts of the site not already in Government ownership. But when the Labour Party was returned to power in February 1974, Camden renewed its opposition, setting out its arguments in an illustrated 32-page, 350mm × 235mm booklet, *Bloomsbury. The case against destruction*, prefaced by letters from the (Labour) Leader of the Council, the (Conservative) Leader of the Minority Party, and from Holborn and St Pancras South's highly influential Labour member of Parliament. Besides arguing in favour of 'a living, diverse community, its future assured because its roots are deep', Camden suggested two other possible sites: the King's Cross railway lands where 'the Library buildings would create an architectural focus' giving an 'atmosphere of quality to a new area', conveniently close to mainline railway stations, tubes and buses, with no need to displace hundreds of people or, alternatively, Covent Garden, 'forming a cultural link with the opera and theatre'.

In reply British Library distributed an academic treatise in miniature, *The Bloomsbury Site for rehousing the Reference Collections of The British Library*, a much more sober and modest 12-page pamphlet, with impeccable arguments appealing to an informed library and information profession, but a non-starter in the Westminster Public Relations and Environment Stakes. Nevertheless it crumbled some of Camden's more sentimental points: 'a visitor to the area, especially at week-ends, will find that the picture of a miniature village humming with life – is very far from correct', claiming that a 'balanced neighbourhood' would result from a new library. Environmental, academic and financial arguments were marshalled in support of 'the national need for a central reference library to hold our unrivalled collections of printed materials and manuscripts...so that tens of thousands of readers, researchers, and visitors from this country and abroad will have easy access to the building'. But, at the end of the day, the cherished site was lost.

Judging that the urgency for a new building was paramount, and that if progress were to be made there should be no further efforts to retain the Bloomsbury site, the British Library Board agreed in December 1974 to examine the feasibility of a new building on a site at Somers Town, on the Euston Road, immediately adjacent to three mainline railway termini. The following August the Board accepted this 9½ acre site on the understanding that 'the detailed design of the new building based on studies already made by the architect would proceed without delay and that construction would start in 1979 if economic conditions at the time permit' ('The New Site', pp.5–6, *Second Annual Report 1974–75*). Early news, comment and a sight of a model prepared by the Department of The Environment as a basis for detailed design, came in 'New Site–decision is final', *British Library News*, No. 1, January 1976:2, 'Feeling of serenity to be lost?', *Library Association Record*, **78**, (2), February 1976:54–5; 'New building at last', *British Library News*, No. 28, April 1978:1–2; 'New British Library building starts next year', *Library Association Record*, **80**, (4), April 1978:148; and 'A library to lead the world', *ibid*.: frontcover and pp.179–82, an illustrated feature plus details of the site, accommodation, form of the building, construction and materials, and the consultants involved.

The first stage of the new building would accommodate the entire Division, thus allowing the national reference collections in the humanities and sciences to be housed together under one roof. Eight general and a number of specialist reading rooms would replace the cramped conditions at Bloomsbury and Holborn. Public facilities would include exhibition areas, a publications shop and a restaurant. All the closed access storage areas would be below ground level, and books would be delivered to the reading rooms by a mechanized handling system. The first stage to be completed would be the SRL block, rare books, and the catalogue hall, with the main printed books section occupying the remaining block if and when approval to go ahead was forthcoming. Four coloured impressions of the frontage, a perspective view, and the model in plan, are inserted between pages 28–9 of the *Fifth Annual Report 1977–78*; two colour photographs of the cleared site and three coloured architect's models appear on pages 53–5, *Sixth Annual Report 1978–79*. A year later the Board impressed upon the Government that the British Library was one of the world's greatest treasure houses of knowledge. Work on the new building should not be delayed: 'without a start on the new building the prospect is one of decay of holdings and services; with it there is the promise of a glorious renaissance of a great institution' (p.9, *Seventh Annual Report 1979–80*).

This seems to have had the desired effect: the Prime Minister, on a visit to Bloomsbury, 28 November 1980, announced the Government's decision to allocate £72 million to the building of the first stage of the new library. On the same day the Minister for the Arts informed the House of Commons of the Government's plans. 'In effect the first phase of the scheme now has been sub-divided into two parts. . .to minimise the cost of the project over the next few critical years but allowing extra storage accommodation, so urgently required, to be made available sooner. . . The second sub-stage would provide further storage accommodation together with a larger degree of associated readers' services' ('Final go-ahead for new building', *British Library News*, No. 60, December 1980:1). As if to celebrate another model of the new building, now being referred to as the St Pancras building, found its way on to the front cover of the *Eighth Annual Report 1980–81*. Concrete evidence of progress came in December 1982 when HRH the Prince of Wales unveiled the foundation stone, commemorated by an illustrated feature 'Library foundation stone unveiled', *British Library News*, No. 81, December 1981:1–2. Three years later, 16 December 1985, the Minister for the Arts informed the Commons of the Government's decision to proceed with the next stage to be completed in 1993 at an estimated cost of £61 million. 'The stage just agreed will provide substantial extra storage space, accommodation for most of the Science Reference and Information Service and reading rooms for western manuscripts and oriental manuscripts and printed books' ('Go ahead for next stage of new Library building', *British Library News*, No. 113, January 1986:1). The first artist's impression of an internal aspect in the new building, the SRIS reading room, appeared on the front cover of the *Thirteenth Annual Report 1985–86*.

With government support forthcoming, with contracts signed, all would appear to be plain sailing to a secure anchorage. But the project was still buffetted by squalls due to a heavy depression hovering over Panizzi's dome-shaped Reading Room. In the Spring of 1979 a group of scholars and writers urged the Secretary for Education to preserve the Reading Room and to reconsider 'the unnecessary new library'. Receiving no encouragement at ministerial level this group launched a Campaign to Save The Reading Room. The case against 'a major, new, all-purpose, science and humanities library', variably and pejoratively described as 'Library City' or 'bibliopolis', was encapsulated in Hugh Thomas' *The case for the reading room*, published as a booklet by the Centre for Policy Studies in June 1983. In detail the new library was opposed on the grounds that it would become a library of first as well as last resort, diluting its role as 'a central source of knowledge and scholastic excellence'. Furthermore, 'The grandiose £300,000,000 new library is neither necessary nor wanted by its readers and is an unnecessary spending of a very large amount of public money'. Instead the Reference Division should remain in the British Museum building, retaining the Reading Room depicted as aesthetically and bibliographically satisfying on all counts. A new depository for 'authorized and new stock' should be built on the designated site and should be connected to Bloomsbury by a tunnel, with mechanized transport for book delivery, enabling books to arrive in the Reading Room 'with no more damage than if [they] were in the same building and perhaps as fast'. Eventually the Newspaper Library at Colindale should be transferred to the new site taking priority over the cultural centre aspect of the new building, the exhibition and restaurant areas, and the seminar and meeting room facilities.

A dissection of the reasons advanced for the urgent necessity for a new library, with a point by point reply, follows explanatory chapters outlining the history of the Bloomsbury and Somers Town projects. The need for more space to house the growing amount of material held at Bloomsbury and its outhouses is acknowledged but it is argued that the kind of building required to hold an increasing number of books is not necessarily the best suited to readers. A comparison is drawn between the comforts of the existing Reading Room as a place of study and research, and air-conditioned storehouses. In fact the author is by no means convinced that every area of the British Library needs to be air-conditioned although recognizing that serious problems need to be tackled. A grave suspicion is voiced that digging a large and deep hole for book storage will cause problems of its own. Overcrowding in the Bloomsbury and Holborn reading rooms is not accepted largely on the evidence of visits to both in October 1979, July 1982 and May 1983 when more than adequate seating was noticed. This may not convince regular users anxiously searching for a vacant seat. The necessity for good working conditions for library staff is acknowledged, but claims that improvements could be made if the Reading Room were to be retained will again cause surprise among those most directly involved. Arguments that a new library building would facilitate more efficient mechanization of library services, or that benefits will accrue from a centralized, multi-discipline library, receive scant sympathy. Planners of the new building are condemned for incorrectly assessing the need and demand amongst Humanities scholars for the new information technologies, and 'the notion that there is a need for one large library to collect all of a nation's knowledge is hardly a self-evident truth: except to enthusiasts for centralisation for its own sake'.

There is a clear inability to regard the British Library as anything other than an extension of the old British Museum Library. It is described as 'a new conglomerate empire, labelled, misleadingly, The British Library'; the Reference Division is a 'misleading and inadequate name' for 'the old established Departments in the Museum'; and 'this complex organization...lumbered what had previously been the British Museum Library with several attachments, whose addition made arguments for a new library more plausible'. Further, 'while this new bibliopolis is being built, the true British Library will remain in the Museum where it always was before its institutional metamorphosis, its heart in the Round Reading Room close to its indispensable adjuncts, the North Library and the Manuscript Room'. What the Campaign is really urging is a return to an exclusively scholarly library unblemished by any contact with users who do not conform to its members' own concept of its aims and purpose: 'The Museum Library has catered for an elite ever since its inception. It must continue so to function.' Whether Antonio Panizzi, for one, would embrace or welcome the view that the BML should remain forever rooted in the middle of the eighteenth century is open to question.

The new building and the eventual evacuation of the Reading Room was a recurrent theme in the quality press. Anthony Sampson's 'A palace of books that nobody needs', *Observer*, 22 July 1979:9 rehearsed many of the arguments found in *The case for the round reading room*; Geoffrey Wheatcroft's 'Why don't we keep the Reading Room?' *Sunday Telegraph*, 11 September 1983 talks extravagantly of 'howls of rage from the library apparatchiki, furious that anything might cheat them of their new plaything'; Gavin Stamp's 'The British Library Thatcher's monument?' *Spectator*, **254**, (8173), 2 March 1985:18–19 reiterates Thomas' arguments and prolonged the improbable hypothesis that the project had prospered despite Government economies, because Sir Frederick (now Lord) Dainton had been one of the the Prime Minister's tutors at Oxford, a proposition repeated in Wheatcroft's 'The British Library – a chapter of accidents', *Daily Telegraph*, 12 January 1987, a clever piece of wordspinning which advanced the debate not an inch. David Hughes' 'Cash probe into super library', *Sunday Times*, 8481, 22 February 1987:4 reports political concern at the new building's escalating costs which were to be referred to the National Audit Office, whilst Stephen Games' 'Books and mortar', *The Independent*, No. 125, 4 March 1987:12 looks at its architectural history. Benjamin Woolley's 'Booking a place for the future', *Listener*, **117**, (3051), 11 June 1987:15–16 reviews the controversy and reveals that one of the Reading Room's ardent defenders had never actually set foot in it. He concludes that 'the temple of knowledge has become the information warehouse, the archive of literature a multi-disciplinary database'. A setback to British Library's hopes was signalled in Robert Hewison's 'Library's unfinished chapters', *Sunday Times*, 20 March 1988:A5 which reported that the St. Pancras building would never be completed as planned because of its prohibitive cost although the present building phase would continue for the next ten years. The Library's Chief Executive was quoted: 'As of today, it's the end of the scheme, and for the foreseeable future'. A measure of comfort and reassurance emerged in a letter from Richard Luce, Minister for the Arts, printed the following week, announcing 'a feasibility study for completing the rest of the building so that the key requirements of the library are met at the minimum additional cost' ('British Library plan will not be shelved', *Sunday Times*, 27 March 1988:B10). A professional perspective is restored in David T. Rogers' 'Alexandria updated: the brief for the British Library building, Euston Road, London', *Aslib Proceedings*, **31**, (7), July 1979:314–21 which elaborates on events from 1970 onwards and distinguishes those factors influencing British Library's planning for differentiated use by its disparate clientele.

Articles in the architectual press have their own fascination. Sherban Cantacuzino's 'A necessary giant', *Architectural Review*, **CLXIV**, (982), December 1978:336–44 comprises a short resume of events, and a brief exposition of architectural principles, followed by a series of architects' and sectional perspectives of the building, axonometrics, coloured sections, and notes on disposition of elements, phasing, structure, services, material and finishes which, cumulatively, expand rather than diminish the mystery of the architect's craft. 'British Library starts on site', *Architects Journal*, **175**, (15), 14 April 1982:56–8 explains the background of the scheme since its inception in 1962 and describes the first stages of excavation and construction. Brian Appleyard's 'Miles of aisles, acres of words', *The Times*, 62679, 30 January 1987:16 reviews the project's architectural history. But the most authoritative voice of all, that of Colin St John Wilson, joint architect of the proposed Great Russell Street building, and given a new brief in 1972 to design a building to meet the needs of British Library and its users well into the 21st century, is embodied in his 'The New Building For The British Library', an IFLA 53rd Council and General Conference, Brighton, August 1987, pre-conference paper, number 16, BUIL/INP/POBL-INF, Division of Management and Technology, Section of Library Building and Equipment. This magisterial overview, essential reading for any study of the new building's design and function, goes into absorbing detail of the brief given him which, in its final form, contained 8000 pieces of information relating to environmental conditions, equipment and spatial parameters, for every Department eventually to be located on the new site. The major factors influencing his design are also explicated: the site's shape and planning requirements, British Library's technical require-ments, and the necessity for a phased building and occupation strategy.

The New British Library Building At St. Pancras, a glossy brochure produced at the end of 1986, and still available, sketches in detail of the site, the brief, some facts and figures, and a calendar of events 1951–91. A rather splendid colour section is concealed inside a folded front cover. Views of the building work in progress were featured in 'The St. Pancras Building', *British Library News,* No. 122, January 1987:2; 'The New British Library Building at St. Pancras', *ibid.,* No. 129, September 1987:2; 'St. Pancras', pp.33–5, *Fourteenth Annual Report 1986–87;* 'The new British Library at St. Pancras', *British Library News,* No. 135, March 1988:1.

Strategic Plan 1985

Even as the British Library was marking its tenth anniversary it was looking forward to developing its services to the library and information profession, to readers, and other users, particularly in the business and industry areas. The commemorative issue of *British Library News*, No. 87, July 1983, ended with the remark 'in anticipation of the availability of accommodation at St. Pancras and of meeting the needs of users in the last decade of the twentieth century, careful planning will be undertaken to make the best use of the resources at our disposal'. And, a year later, delivering a paper at the Library Association conference in Bournemouth, Kenneth Cooper, Chief Executive of the Library, seized the opportunity to float what he described as 'one or two ideas which in collaboration with colleagues I shall hope to drop in the ferment of ideas which already characterizes the Library in ways and at times that will help us to move on'. Specifically, he declared, 'it is time for the British Library to have a corporate plan'. Not that planning had been ignored or neglected during the Library's comparatively short existence: 'How could it have successfully developed so much of its work and so many of its services?' But, despite a good deal of forward planning, 'this has not so far fed through to the Board in the systematic way that will certainly be needed in future to enable the best decisions to be taken between competing priorities'. Reduced resources, continuing financial restraints, intensifying 'the problems of choosing between what might go forward, what can wait and what may be discontinued', demanded 'a clearer statement, an up-to-date statement of our objectives and of the future plans that flow from them'. In essence 'a carefully prepared corporate plan for the Library will be of significant help to management and staff throughout the organization in the coming years'. Not only would such a document 'provide an important basis for future dialogue between the Library and the Office of Arts and Libraries' but it would also benefit everyone else in the library world.

The crucial management dilemmas confronting the British Library, the import of which was perhaps scarcely heeded or noticed at the time, were expressed in the form of two key questions: 'How do we reconcile best service to today's users with our responsibility to preserve the national collections for future generations?' and 'Where does the balance lie between raising revenue through charging for services and rupturing a tradition of freedom of information which has arguably been a key constituent in the nurture and growth of scholarship?' ('The view from the top: a corporate plan for the BL', *Library Association Record*, **86**, (10), October 1984:414).

How the British Library Board perceived the way forward was revealed when *Advancing With Knowledge. The British Library Strategic Plan 1985–1990*, a 40-page A4 size booklet, was published in October 1985. A brief version, a six-page folded pamphlet, with an identical cover, is available *gratis* from Press and Public Relations, The British Library, 2 Sheraton Street, London W1V 4BH. Slightly amended this featured as an insert in *Library Association Record*, **87**, (11), November 1985. The decision to publish the Plan in full was prompted by a desire that all staff of the Library might better understand how their own individual work contributed to the Library's operations overall, and also by the recognition that the British Library was the largest of the many institutions forming the national library network. Any substantial change in the British Library's operation would inevitably affect the policies and practices of other institutions.

A review of the British Library's responsibilities and activities 'across the broad sweep of academic and business needs' occupies the first two chapters, two momentous paragraphs framing the whole purpose of this strategic document:

> Sustaining this great Library and all the benefits it offers into the future will demand adequate resources and clear-sighted management. The resources needed to maintain the collections and services at their present levels rise faster than the official rate of inflation, largely because world publications increase in

volume and foreign items increase in price even more rapidly. At the same time developments in information technology and pressures for easy and efficient access to the growing storehouse of information and knowledge are raising expectations of library and information services.

The Board therefore thought it timely to reconsider the whole range of its policies and to set out a clear structure for the future. The Strategic Plan which follows is the product of an intensive process of consultation and deliberation between the Board members and management in all parts of the Library, and should be seen as an agenda for action and policy making in the years immediately ahead. It will need to be reviewed periodically in the light of changing conditions' (paras 1.6 and 1.7, p.9).

The inexorable growth in availability and demand for information, especially in the financial, economic and business areas, 'places an emphasis on up-to-date, accurate and quantitative information 'whilst developments in information technology raise 'fundamental questions concerning the future roles and relationships between the leading participants in the library and information sector'. These developments will stimulate a major growth in electronic publishing; bibliographic and source databases will expand electronic document ordering and delivery services; and micropublishing, 'in which digitised text of publications distributed on compact, low-cost physical media will grow in importance. . .as a cost-effective means of publishing bulk text and illustrations, where there is a premium on convenience and rapid searching'. The British Library is planning positively and flexibly to fact these challenges: '(i) major new market opportunities are emerging that the Library is well placed to serve; (ii) the Library's central position as a supplier of documents of first and last resort, and as the national printed archive, is reinforced by financial constraints on U.K. libraries; (iii) continued investment in information technology is critical for future cost effective provision; (iv) the Library needs to develop its management and marketing skills while continuing to nurture the high standards of professionalism and scholarship which have made it one of the world's great research libraries' (para 2.12, p.12).

Three key strategies are disclosed to fulfil the Library's aims and objectives:

(i) a fundamental commitment to the programme for the new Library building at St. Pancras, which is designed to provide an integrated, modern facility for the future National Library services;

(ii) a corporate approach to the management of the Library's collections, from acquisition to preservation. This will aim to provide the widest possible national-level collection in support of service objectives;

(iii) a major thrust towards developing a programme of wider service provision, both through increased access to the collections and the development of revenue-generating services. Increasingly, services will be focussed more sharply on meeting the needs of particular user groups' (para 3.5, p.14).

Chapter 5, 'Collection Management', reports what is rather than projecting a radical what will be, the emphasis is on the continuation of sound and well-established practices, even to an assurance that 'the Library is not looking at present to extend its own collecting activities' although it will be developing proposals for extending legal deposit and bibliographic coverage of non-book materials, to microforms and the whole new area of electronic publications. 'We see a particularly strong case for the development of the Library's role as the national archival centre for electronic publications, building on its current involvement with digital mapping and proposals for access to patents in digital form' (paras 5.20–5.21, pp.20–21). In the field of record creation the main trend will be away from the production of microfiche and printed outputs towards online catalogue access and online cataloguing.

A statement that 'the Library exists for the benefit of its users both now and in the future, and the fuller satisfaction of user requirements is a key motive for our operations and developments' introduces a sixth chapter on Services. Because services depend on revenue other than Treasury grant-in-aid, 'charging policies in relation to different kinds of service provision' have been examined in addition to the scope for developing more services. A Corporate Marketing Manager appointment has been created 'to reinforce and develop more widely marketing expertise across the Library'. In considering how its services should be funded the

Library had divided its activities into three broad categories: 'public good' collections to be funded out of grant-in-aid income; services which exploit the 'public good' asset for the widest possible benefit, usually supporting the national library and information network, where the level of charging will depend on policy considerations; and value added services, involving high staff costs, which will be administered on a cost-recovery basis. 'We shall be using this framework to draw out the principles underpinning the Library's charging policies for its major services as a basis for ensuring realistic financial targets and better allocation of resources' (para 6.7, p.23). Charging readers for admission to the collections had been considered but had been rejected. 'It is clear that significant charges would have to be imposed on regular users...to offer prospects of yielding even as much as £250,000 a year. We set that against the civilised tradition of free access for researchers for public knowledge which is deeply rooted in Britain and the vast majority of other countries, and which could not well be breached without serious repercussions on the Library's relations with its main users' (para 6.8, p.24). It is not clear which of these two factors proved decisive, it may be charging was only mentioned as a sop to the prevailing Government's financial philosophy.

Chapter 7 'Relationships With The Library And Information Network' also contains little that is new: the Library will keep under regular review...continue to play a major role...pursue opportunities...foster bilateral relationships...continue to participate.... It is hard to avoid the somewhat cynical conclusion that much of this heavily jargonized exposition of the Library's activities is intended for Whitehall, Westminster and Downing Street consumption. Rather more substantial is the 'Support of Research and Development' section where three leading issues have been identified to influence and guide the research programme: (i) the application and implementation of information technology for library and information services; (ii) the implications of information being treated much more than hitherto as a tradeable commodity; (iii) the effects of economic and social constraints on library and information services' (para 7.20, p.32). Related priority areas for support over the next five years are industrial, business and commercial information research; information policy research, including library policy and the economics of information; and basic and strategic information research examining underlying principles of information storage and retrieval.

The problems afflicting any large organization, management, staff development, corporate responsibility for key services, integrated development of systems for planning and financial management, consultation with appropriate unions, the planning of automation to improve efficiency in all spheres of its operations, the avoidance of proliferation of incompatible microcomputer systems and facilities, take up the bulk of chapter 8, 'Organisation And Resource Strategy'. Of broader interest than these domestic preoccupations is the Library's future funding which will continue to depend on the success of efforts 'to improve productivity, to increase revenue, to work in partnership with the private sector and to attract private sponsorship, as well as on the readiness of Government in practice to maintain the value of the annual grant-in-aid in real terms'. A plain warning is given that any weakening of Government commitment would inevitably undermine determination within the Library to take full advantage of revenue and sponsorship opportunities. In the best of circumstances 'there is likely to be sustained pressure throughout the period on the total resources available to the Library; optimum achievements will demand flexible and imaginative development and implementation of the many and varied elements of the plan' (para 8.21, p.37). The message is clear: if the British Library is to function at full throttle then it must be adequately resourced; the whole purpose of the publication of *Advancing With Knowledge*, proclaiming the value of its services to the nation as never before, revolved around driving that message home. Certainly it was the theme the Chief Executive returned to at the press conference held to launch the plan:

> If we get plus two per cent on the grant in aid, as we are promised at the moment, then we shall have to find further economies in our acquisition of material and documentation plans, though it is not possible to say where these economies will fall.
>
> If this sort of funding pattern went on for a prolonged period of years, however, the national collection as represented by the Library, the collection of last resort for libraries, then its holding

would become seriously depleted.

If we are serious about making progress in economic and cultural terms as a knowledge based society, then surely we ought to get at least average division in the total allocation of public expenditure. At least average, that is all we are asking for.

We are saying to the Government, if you give us that we will contend with the various variables, the rising cost of literature material, and the problems of exchange rates which inevitably afflict us.

In the meantime the Library would not attempt to plan budgets in detail on a quinquennial basis, instead operational plans would be formulated to achieve set targets. Economies would be found by closing down the Manchester bindery, developing common stock, and by the automation of serials processing. Existing revenue earning services would be set targets and some proposed new services, such as computer information searching for business enquiries, would be expected to be self-financing. Publishing ventures and the production of a national discography would be financed with private sector sponsorship. Core developments like BLAISE-LINE 2, and a new telecommunications network would continue to be funded from Treasury grant-in-aid.

British Library News, No. 111, September/October 1985 described *Advancing With Knowledge* as 'a working document for management and staff and an information document for the library and information community'. In the same issue the appointment is announced of the Library's first Corporate Marketing Manager with a brief 'to increase the Library's revenue from non-Government sources, to improve the quality of the Library's services and to represent effectively to Government and the taxpayer the Library's value to the nation'. No doubt the strategic plan has its uses as a working document for British Library staff, it unquestionably explains the Library's operations in detail to the library profession, but the true purpose of *Advancing With Knowledge* is to alert Government that economies can only go so far and that if a truly effective service to scholarship and industry is required, then it must be adequately resourced. N. Macartney's 'The British Library Strategic Plan', *Journal of Librarinaship,* **18**, (2), 1986:133–42, subjects it to detailed scrutiny.

Nouvelles de la dernière heure

Strategic planning, a massive but controversial new home for its London-based collections, conversion of the *General Catalogue* to machine-readable form, new storage accommodation at Boston Spa, SRIS's introduction of its Japanese Information Service, the National Sound Archive's CEDAR project, all recounted in preceding chapters, bear impressive witness that the British Library is a dynamic rather than a dormant institution. But even these definitive projects, either contracted or nearing completion, do not present a rounded picture of current initiatives or activities.

In February 1988 Document Supply Centre officially launched the ADONIS project, a trial document delivery service that supplies 219 biomedical journals published 1987–88 on CD-ROM. Biomedicine was the discipline chosen because the demand for recent biomedical articles is heavier than for other areas. ADONIS was established by an international consortium of science serials publishers (Blackwell Scientific Publications, Pergamon, Elsevier and Springer Verlag) concerned lest the operation of the 'fair use' clause of copyright legislation by organizations supplying photocopies of journal articles should depress their circulation figures. If new technology could satisfy requests more cheaply than conventional high cost, labour intensive photocopying procedures, the monies saved could be shared with the copyright holders at no extra expense to the user. The journal contents are indexed by Excerpta Medica in Amsterdam to provide a bibliographic record for each article, which is then identified by a unique ADONIS number, the journal articles are scanned, the index data and the scanned images are merged, and a master CD-ROM disc is pressed. At ten day intervals copies of new discs are despatched to 13 major document delivery centres in Europe,

North America, Mexico, Japan and Australia. The full background of ADONIS including future developments, its advantages and disadvantages, is outlined in David Bradbury's 'ADONIS–The View Of The Users' and Barrie T. Stern's 'ADONIS: The Experience To Date', pre-conference papers for IFLA's 53rd Council & General Conference, Brighton, August 1987, Paper 23, SCIE/SER-SCIE, Division of Special Libraries and Division of Collections and Services, Section of Science And Technological Libraries and Section of Serial Publications. An illustrated brochure, *ADONIS The Facts*, is available from DSC or P.O. Box 2400, 1000 CK Amsterdam. 'Discovering the future', *DSC Newsletter*, No. 13, September 1987:1; 'ADONIS Launch', *British Library News*, No. 135, March 1988:2; and 'A New Era', *Document Supply News*, No. 15, March 1988:1 carry further detail.

Boston Spa is also one of the main information providers to the Commission of European Communities APOLLO project (Article Procurement With On-Line Local Ordering), a high-speed data transmission system by which documents are requested and retrieved electronically but with the actual document delivery being by conventional methods. DSC demonstrated APOLLO's potential at Boston Spa in January 1987. 'Digitalized pages from a variety of documents were transmitted the 25,000 miles to the EUTELSAT ECS F-2 satellite, launched by the European Space Agency in 1984 and stationed over French Guyana, and then bounced back and printed out. The quality of the copy received is markedly better than the current (Group III) FAX methods' ('Documents Through Space', *DSC Newsletter*, No. 10, March 1987:1). The background to APOLLO, a technical description, its economic implications, and its future are all treated in David Bradbury's 'Apollo: Document Delivery By Satellite', a pre-conference paper, IFLA 53rd Council & General Conference, Brighton, August 1987, Paper 20, SPEC/ART/ART-AVM/ADM, Division of Special Libraries and Division of Management and Technology, Section Of Administrative Libraries.

A review of British Library's policy on the acquisition and retention of materials was initiated in 1987 to make a strategic assessment of the implications of the current collecting policies for meeting the future needs of researchers, and for providing adequate storage beyond the year 2000. The review team is to examine the priorities underlying existing policies on acquisition and permanent retention, to consider the case for a revision of those priorities and what they would imply, the case for and against imposing a ceiling on the growth of British Library lending stock bearing in mind British Library's services and revenue and the cost-effectiveness of UK libraries generally, and policy developments on common stock which any ceiling on lending stock growth might require. The review team, led by Dr Brian Enright, has been asked to report by December 1988. 'Review of Acquisition and Retention Policies: an interim report', *British Library News*, No. 136, April 1988:1 raises the fundamental question whether all items currently deposited under the copyright regulations are appropriate for the national library's collections. If this theme is pursued it will devastate the last resort concept.

Bibliographic Services is investigating networking BLAISE RECORDS in the widest possible context, mounting the HMSO file, and linking with external databases, including the cooperative cataloguing systems. Research and Development awarded a grant of £41,200 for an 18-month project, starting in October 1987, *The Bibliographic Control of Computer Files: the Feasibility Of Creating a National Catalogue*. Two areas of research are anticipated: the project's software requirements and the application of standard library cataloguing procedures to the cataloguing of computer files. The likely benefits of such a national catalogue include a better service for users of computer files by facilitating their location, identification and access; the introduction of standard in-house control procedures, an increase in the use of computer files, and improvements in computer file documentation.

To maximize its efforts in attracting sponsors a 'central focus' has been established in the Chief Executive's office to develop a corporate strategy for sponsorship; draw up a programme of likely projects; collect and disseminate information on projects, sponsors and contacts; advise on proposed applications for funding to companies and trusts; and to monitor progress. Future plans emphasize attracting money from commercial companies and five areas have been identified where sponsorship might supplement resources: the development of the Library's facilities, exhibitions, the acquisition and preservation of special collections, publishing and the enhancement of services.

British Library's own reservoir of technical, bibliographical and management expertise has not been neglected. A Consultancy

Services Unit, set up at Boston Spa, will market this expertise. Overseas governments and institutions are invited to call upon British Library's expert advice and support in all aspects of library and information service development. Its first contract was to aid the setting up of a Gulf Studies Centre in the Emirate of Sharjah and subsequently the Director of the National Sound Archive advised on the design of its auditorium and exhibition area. A coloured pictorial leaflet, *The Consultancy Services Of The British Library,* introduces their scope with special reference to the Library's experience in collection and services development, effective management and in applying modern information technology.

High on British Library's priority list is raising the proportion of its total expenditure earned from revenue from 22 per cent to 25 per cent by 1990. Increasingly it is looking to joint projects with private companies. A prime example is the Nineteenth Century project undertaken in association with Chadwyck-Healey and other research libraries in the UK and USA. Expected to last for the next 30 years, and to earn a considerable sum of money, this involves republishing on microfiche books and pamphlets regarded as essential texts in one large General Collection covering history and the social sciences and a number of separately available specialist collections in linguistics, art and architecture, publishing and the book trade, and music. A publishing programme with Harvester Press Microform Publications Ltd is expected to continue. Already three series of *British Literary Manuscripts from the British Library London* have been issued on 35mm silver-halide positive microfilm: *The English Renaissance: Literature from the Tudor Period to the Restoration c1500–c1700; The Eighteenth Century, c1700–c1800;* and *The Medieval Age c1150–c1500.* Other projects with Harvester include *Medieval Literary and Historical Manuscripts in the Cotton Collection; The Literary Manuscripts of William Morris; The English Stage after the Restoration;* and *Nineteenth Century Theatre Periodicals.*

To improve the effectiveness of its publishing operations a working party, chaired by Timothy Rix, Chief Executive of the Longman Group and a member of the British Library Board, was formed early in 1987 charged with the task of defining a publishing policy that will serve the Library's needs for the next ten years and to report by the Autumn. Options the working party was expected to explore included the setting up of a limited liability company or a centralized publishing unit under a Publications Officer. Its deliberations would be taking place against the background of an existing publishing programme which in 1986 generated almost £3½ million, by no means a neglible sum, especially as British Library does not enjoy its own retail outlet.

A major project comes to fruition in the summer of 1988 when a *Location Register Of Twentieth-Century English Literary Manuscripts And Letters: a union list of papers of modern English, Irish, Scottish and Welsh authors in the British Isles* is published in two volumes. Based on a research project at the University of Reading Library, the *Register* aims to record the location of all such material known to be available for consultation in the British Isles and is expected to contain over 50,000 entries. Details of coverage and production methods are printed in *BS Newsletter*, No. 44, October 1987:5.

Appendices

Appendix A

British Library General Publications

Section 4(3) of *The British Library Act 1972* stipulates that 'The Board shall, not later than such date in each year as the Secretary of State may determine, send to him a report of the proceedings and activities of the Board during the previous twelve months, and the Secretary of State shall lay copies of the report before each House of Parliament'. When a full-scale history of the British Library comes to be written these *Annual Reports* will offer important insights into what was preoccupying the Board, and what it wanted to call Parliament's attention to at any given moment. Naturally no opportunity is lost to blazon the Library's progress and achievements but the *Reports* are by no means simply how-we-do-it-good bulletins. Difficulties are not glossed over whether they concern the grading of junior staff or a serious service deficiency. From time to time that hoary old circumlocution this or that department continues to. . .is given an airing but, in general, the *Reports* are sharply to the point.

The first nine *Reports* grew steadily in size: 16 pages was sufficient for 1973–4, 99 pages were necessary for 1981–2. In truth they were all very worthy but a trifle dull. A distinct change in style, content and presentation was apparent in the *Tenth Annual Report 1982–83*:

Partly to symbolise the fusion into a corporate entity of the component units from which the Library was constituted and partly to enable readers to gain a more coherent appreciation of the Library and its activities this Annual Report differs in form from its predecessors. The first part presents a corporate view, ignoring the Divisional and Departmental boundaries, whilst the various schedules and appendices which comprise

161

the second part provide statistical information and the names of some of those outside the Library who help it through their work on the British Library Advisory Council, the five Advisory Committees and various working parties (p.8).

Notably acquisitions, publications during the year, and a selected list of articles about the Library not restricted to those actually printed in the year under review, are also printed. Unfortunately for the historian or bibliographer this list is confined to articles in professional journals, and is not extended to more ephemeral items in the daily or weekly press. The simultaneous transformation of the *Reports* into sumptuously illustrated A4 glossy, 60-page books has been both startling and aesthetically gratifying. They have now become collectors' items in their own right.

British Library News, an (almost) monthly newssheet, first circulated in January 1976, is addressed primarily to library management and senior librarians. Its aim is to present news and information about the British Library as a whole and it supplements the various divisional newsletters, sometimes carrying abstracts of items previously printed in those more specialized publications. Regular features include news of staff activities, notes on new publications, exhibitions and new initiatives and developments. 'Around and about the British Library', a series which turned the spotlight on various sections and departments earlier in the decade was especially informative and could profitably be updated and repeated.

'Scholarly yet readable' were the editor's watchwords when *The British Library Journal* started in 1975. Whether or not the scholarship is readable to the uninitiated layman may be open to doubt but clearly the *Journal* reflects the British Library Board's determination that the traditional erudition which is the legacy of the British Museum shall not entirely disappear in the maelstrom of change and reorganization. Each issue, annual to 1983, twice yearly subsequently, contains learned and authoritative articles on books and manuscripts already in the collections; lists and accounts of important new acquisitions of older items; and shorter notices by staff and readers. A cumulative index every ten years is expected.

For the first 13 issues (1984–6) *Focus* represented the views of senior management. Much of its content was of domestic interest only but it nevertheless afforded an unparalleled insight into British Library affairs. A stern resolve not to refer to it in the preceding chapters on the grounds that it was a privately circulated publication, and relatively inaccessible, was relaxed on only one occasion. With the December 1986 issue *Focus* changed its character: it is now a staff newsletter pure and simple, still informative but more journalistic in style and appearance. The emphasis is now on people rather than grave policy issues, the previous unrelieved columns of closely printed text have given way to widely spaced news snippets interspersed with illustrations and cartoons.

British Library Occasional Papers
Consist mainly of printed proceedings of British Library colloquia.

Titles
1. *Canadian Studies*. Papers presented at a colloquium in August 1983. 1985.
2. *Library Publishing*. Papers presented at a conference in April 1983. 1985.
3. Ian Willison: *National Research Librarianship*, 1987.
4. *Australian and New Zealand Studies*. Papers presented at a colloquium in February 1984. 1985.
5. *Bibliography and the Study of 15th-Century Civilisation*. Papers presented at a colloquium in September 1984. 1987.
6. *African Studies*. Papers presented at a colloquium in January 1985. 1986.
7. *South Asian Studies*. Papers presented at a colloquium in April 1985. 1986.
8. *German Studies*. Papers presented at a colloquium in September 1985. 1986.
9. *Musical Pursuits*. Selected essays by Alec Hyatt King. 1987.
10. *Chinese Studies*. Papers presented at a colloquium in August 1987. 1988.

Two brochures were issued in the summer of 1987. *The British Library*, a 12-page illustrated pamphlet, introduces its multifarious collections and services, and includes directory-type information and some general facts and figures. *The British Library Serving the World* is a more elaborate brochure, directed at overseas users, describing in greater detail the Library's services and how to exploit them. To the conservative home reader its language might sound a trifle bombastic but this simply reflects the entrepreneurial spirit which now imbues British Library's corporate marketing and sponsorship office. It is balanced by the becoming modesty of the word 'almost' in its opening sentence: 'The British Library has almost certainly the most varied and exciting collections of any library in the world.' A pocket inside the back cover accommodates a set of leaflets currently including *The British Library National Sound Archive; BLAISE-LINE Order! A Fast And Effective Document Supply Service; BLAISE Records—The New British Library Record Supply Service; BLDSC Use of Facsimile Transmission; BLDSC and ADONIS Document Supply from CD-ROM; Science Reference And Information Service;* and *The Consultancy Services of The British Library,* and a multilingual introduction to the Library. Revised in October 1987, *A Brief Guide To Some Libraries In London,* a single sheet folded into eight A5 pages, is issued by Humanities And Social Sciences Information and Admissions Section. The resources of 46 public and specialized libraries are indicated.

All British Library published titles in print are listed in *British Library Publications. New Titles & Complete List.* A detailed section on new titles is followed by a complete list of new and backlist titles. All entries give author, title, date, pagination, size, format, ISBN or ISSN and price. Editorial and marketing information, and notes on how to order, are to be found inside the front cover.

Appendix B

British Library Lectures and Concerts

British Library Annual Research Lectures
Each year R & D sponsor a distinguished speaker to deliver a lecture on a major topic in librarianship or information science to an invited audience. The lectures are subsequently printed in a glossy 295 × 180mm soft covered format and are available *gratis* on application.

Titles
1982 Murray Laver: *Information technology and libraries.*
1983 Alexander King: *The coming information society.*
1984 Frederick C. Kilgour: *Beyond bibliography.*
1985 Sir Harry Hookway: *Can knowledge survive?*
1986 Jean-Claude Gardin: *Expert systems and scholarly publications.*
1987 Neil McLean: *Open Systems–Open Market.*

The Panizzi Lectures
These annual lectures were established in 1984 to honour Sir Anthony Panizzi, the renowned nineteenth-century Principal Librarian. They are based on original research in bibliography or related areas and are published in soft covers.

Titles
1985 D. A. Mackenzie: *Bibliography and the sociology of texts.*
1986 T. A. Birrell: *English monarchs and their books: from Henry VII to Charles II.*
1987 Kenneth Humphreys: *A National Library: In Theory and in practice.*

Dainton Lecture
Initiated by Science, Technology and Industry division in honour of Lord Dainton who himself gave the first lecture to an invited audience at the Royal Society, 30 March 1987, on 'Knowledge is power: but how can we find what we want?' The 1988 lecture was given by W. Gordon Graham on The Future of Scientific Publishing.

British Library Zweig Series
The Stefan Zweig series of lectures and concerts marks the gift to the Library of a collection of some 180 musical and literary manuscripts by the Trustees of the Stefan Zweig collection, the most important and most generous gift the British Library has received since its formation. The 40-page, A4 souvenir programme of the first concert series, *Stefan Zweig Series of Concerts, Lectures And Exhibitions April-May 1987*, contains essays on 'Stefan Zweig 1881–1942' and 'Musical autographs in the Zweig Collection' by Oliver Neighbour and 'Literary Autographs' by Pamela Porter. There is a preliminary list of all manuscripts in the Collection although it is anticipated that further research may result in a more detailed identification of some items. 'The Library is taking the opportunity provided by the impetus of the Zweig gift to start a programme of live music based on its collections to become an established part of its activities over the next few years' (Introduction). 'The British Library Stefan Zweig Series 1988', *British Library News*, No. 134, February 1988:1 reports that the aim of the second series is to bring together the musical and literary aspects of the Zweig collection.

Appendix C

Two Supporters Clubs

The American Trust for the British Library was formed in 1979. Its primary objective was to fill gaps in the Library's collections of American materials published during the period 1880–1950 when grants for the purchase of such material were exiguous. It also directed its efforts to replacing the 9,000 American books destroyed by bombing during the Second World War. The Trust assists the Library in other ways 'by encouraging owners of important private collections to give the British Library the opportunity to acquire items and by acting as a go-between between the British Library and American booksellers' ('British Library to benefit from American Trust', *British Library News*, No. 61, January/February 1981:1).

Douglas W. Bryant's 'The American Trust for the British Library', *Harvard Library Bulletin*, **29**, (3), July 1981:298–306 narrates the British Museum Library's nineteenth-century efforts to build up its American collections, primarily through the agency of Henry Stevens, the Vermont bookseller, and the postwar expansion of American Studies courses in British universities which highlighted the need to reinforce the retrospective holdings of the British Library. A 12-page brochure issued in 1985, *The American Trust for the British Library*, covers much the same ground and gives an impressive report of its fund raising operations 1979 to date. News of British Library's activities and publications, and its own successes in attracting major grants, are printed in an occasional *Newsletter* whose first issue was dated Fall 1980.

A Friends of the British Library organization to encourage, assist and promote the work of the Library was announced late in 1987. Its aims will be (1) 'to widen public understanding of the British Library through the provision of information on its collections and services;' (2) 'to improve awareness of the Library's role as a cultural centre and a guardian of the national heritage;' (3) 'to provide a means of developing special relationships with the private sector for fund raising and joint venture activities;' and (4) 'to establish itself as a self financing revenue and profile raising organisation over a period of two to three years' ('Friends of the British Library to be set up,' *British Library News*, No. 131, November 1987:1). The scheme is to be launched in June 1988.

Appendix D

Addresses and Admission

Humanities and Social Sciences
English Language, Western and European collections of printed books; Official Publications and Social Sciences; Western Manuscripts; Map Library; Music collections; and Philatelic collections. Also Preservation Service. Great Russell Street, London WC1B 3DG.

Oriental Collections, Store Street, London WC1E 7DG.

India Office Library and Records, 197 Blackfriars Road, London SE1 8NG.

British Library Information Sciences Service, 7 Ridgmount Street, London WC1E 7AE.

Newspaper Library, Colindale Avenue, London NW9 5HE.

National Sound Archive, 29 Exhibition Road, London SW7 2AS.

Bibliographic Services
2 Sheraton Street, London W1V 4BH.

Science, Technology and Industry
Document Supply Centre, Boston Spa, Wetherby, West Yorkshire LS23 7BQ.

Science Reference and Information Service, 25 Southampton Buildings, Chancery Lane, London WC2A 1AW and 9 Kean Street, London WC2B 4AT.

Research and Development Department
2 Sheraton Street, London W1V 4BH.

Admission to the General Reading Room, North Library, North Library Gallery, Official Publications and Social Sciences Service, at Bloomsbury, and the Oriental Reading Room and the India Office Library is by a photographic pass obtainable from Reader Admission Office, Great Russell Street, London WC1B 3DG. Details are in *Applying for a Reader's Pass*. A supplementary pass is needed for the Manuscripts Students Room. No pass is required by Science Reference and Information Service or for use in Document Supply Centre's reading room (contact The Reading Room, Document Supply Centre, Boston Spa, Wetherby, West Yorkshire LS23 7BQ). The Listening Service at the National Sound Archive is by appointment. Two pocket laminated cards *The Reading Rooms and Times of Opening* and *Document Supply Centre Useful Contact Numbers* are available.

Appendix E

Select bibliography 1974–1987

The British Library' (editorial), *Aslib Proceedings*, **26**, (5), May 1974: 168–176. Includes an annotated list of the major papers relative to the formation of the British Library from 1971.

Woodward, K. R., *The British Library. A bibliography*, Coventry, Cadig Liaison Centre, 1974.

Saunders, W. L. ed., *British Librarianship Today*, Library Association, 1976. Chapters 4–8 cover the British Library.

Higham, N., 'The impact of the British Library on the national and international scene', *Aslib Proceedings*, **31**, (2), February 1979:97–106.

Lunn, A., *BNB/BSD 1949–1979 Thirty Years of bibliographic achievement*, British Library Bibliographic Services Division, 1979.

Polden, A. G., 'The British Library', *International Library Review*, **12**, (3), July 1980:269–285.

Journal of Documentation, **37**, (3), September 1981 and **37**, (4), December 1981: Bloomfield, B. C., 'The British Library 1973–80', Sep 1981:107–124; Urquhart, D. J., 'Some Thoughts On The British Library', Sep 1981:125–133; Simpson, N., 'The British Library: A Public Librarian's View', Dec 1981:157–165; Gatt, J. E., 'The British Library And The Shire County', Dec 1981:166–170; Ayres, F. H., 'The British Library And The University Library', Dec 1981:171–177; Revill, D. H., 'The British Library: A Polytechnic Perspective', Dec 1981:178–179; Simkins, M. A., 'The British Library And Industrial Research Libraries', Dec 1981:187–192.

Wilson, A., 'The incorporation of the British Museum Library into the British Library', *in* Vaughan, A., *Studies in Library Management Vol 7*, Clive Bingley, 1982.

Library Review, 32, Spring 1983. A Library Review Revision Study.

Jones, G., 'The Making Of The British Library', pp.8–31
Revell, P., 'Reference Division', pp.32–44.
Day, A. E., 'Lending Division', pp.45–63.
Jeffreys, A. E., 'Bibliographic Services Division', pp.66–77.
Whiteman, P., 'Research and Development Department', pp.79–109.
Barr, K. P., 'The British Library Lending Division: The First Ten Years', *Interlending and Document Supply*, **11**, (3), July 1983: 79–92.
Wilson, A., 'Developments in cooperation between the British Library Reference Division and other libraries and information centres', *Journal of Librarianship*, **15**, (3), July 1983:155–168.
Anderson, J., *The British Library. The Reference Division Collections*, British Library, 1983.
Encyclopaedia of Library and Information Science Vol 36. Supplement 1. New York, Marcel Dekker, 1983. The British Library, pp.54–91.
Roberts, E. F. D., 'The British Library: directions and locations', *TLS*, No 4218, 3 February 1984:110 & 123.
Guide to Government Department and other libraries. British Library Science Reference and Information Service, 27e, 1985.
Line, M. B. ed., *The World of Books and Information. Essays In Honour Of Lord Dainton*, The British Library, 1987.
Essays of immediate relevance include Kenneth Cooper's 'The British Library–an organization for others' (pp.45–58); Michael Hill's 'From reference library to information service: a review of the changing role of the Science Reference and Information Service' (pp.119–127); and Sir Peter Swinnerton-Dyer's 'The evolution of the British Library's research policy' (pp.179–185).
State of the Art of the Applications of New Information Technologies in Libraries and their impact on Library Functions in the United Kingdom. Library and Information Technology Centre, 1987. The British Library pp.36–42.

Index

174

179

189